£1-75

West Riding Engineman

Steam Shunters to High-Speed Train

by
Bill Addy

Dalesman Books
1984

The Dalesman Publishing Company Ltd.
Clapham, via Lancaster, LA2 8EB

First published 1984

© Bill Addy, 1984

ISBN: 0 85206 766 6

Phototypeset, printed and bound by Galava Printing Co. Ltd., Nelson, Lancashire

Contents

Front cover photograph of 5MT No. 44965 and B1 No. 61406 at Leeds Holbeck shed on March 29th, 1965, by Gavin Morrison

Introduction

I COME from a railway family. My father was a driver at Stourton locomotive depot, Leeds, and retired with 47 years' service. My mother worked in the carriage shops at Derby as a french polisher up to getting married, and all the family on her side have — and still do — work in differing branches on the railway at Derby. I was reared among the back-to-back houses of Hunslet, until I was married, and lived in the shadow of the 'slag' wall of the old Leeds Steel Works; the wall was about thirty feet in height and surrounded the works. High above our street was a buffer stop — or a dead-end — where the works locomotive backed up to have a run up to the furnaces with about four wagons of scrap. The times we stood as kids watching and hoping to see it come too far and end up in our street!

The dirt and dust that covered our houses daily was quite something. It was a dirty white substance and was also of a caustic nature, and every window in the surrounding area had no glaze left on the outside — a yellow duster would cling to it unaided. Within a couple of hours of sweeping the floors there would be enough dust in the doorway to write in it. But this did not deter my mother and the other womenfolk from standing fresh-baked oven-cakes, the size of dinner plates, on their edges on a sheet of newspaper in the doorway to cool. When cool enough a new cake was never cut but instead one tore a piece off and smeared it with "Maggie Ann" margarine whilst it was still warm — lovely! Like most homes in Hunslet we had a dog, a great shaggy lovable mongrel which used to brush past the new cake on its way in and out. Germs were unknown to us and we never suffered as a consequence.

My main introduction to steam engines was not railway ones but road steam engines. Pepper Road which passed our street-end led to several large engineering works, such as Henry Berry and Clayton's boiler makers, Mann's Patent Flue & Tube Works and others. Most of them had steam lorries for their heavy haulage, almost all of which stopped at a hydrant at the end of the street to fill up and clean the fires; they had thick solid tyres the same as fairground tractors.

Apart from the heavy industry, there was also a large cemetery at the top of Pepper Road and about three-quarters of the funerals passed our street. This was a 'heaven-sent' opportunity for the women to find fresh gossip; my mum was no exception, by noting who was in which carriage and who was still with who. The carriages were immaculate and very highly polished and really sparkled; they were drawn by equally well turned-out jet black horses, one to each coach and two to the hearse. The coaches also served for weddings with the addition of a length of white silk ribbon. I came home one day and found the women standing in a group at the street-end as usual; there was a funeral procession approaching. As I got to them, I heard one say, 'They're burying Mary Lightowler today!' And someone else, 'Ee is that right? Is she dead?' I burst out laughing but was quickly shut up by my mother—this was serious business.

In hindsight this was an interesting era. The coalman delivered coal from the cart from a large scoop slung at the back; the milk was brought in large churns straight from the farms and ladled into the housewives' basins. I have even bought jam from local shops—back-to backs with a counter at the back of the door—spooned into a cup from a big jar with a large wooden spoon.

I left school at fourteen without any preconceived idea of what job I wanted; it was 1932 so it was more a case of what jobs were available. For the last remaining weeks prior to leaving, I and a few other lads spent our Saturday mornings dashing round the engineering works and factories in the district asking for work but without much success. Eventually I managed to get a job making Silver Cross prams, but as was the practice in most engineering industries in those days, when you got in front with your work you were laid off without pay until they caught up and would then send for you back. It happened to me once, but when they sent for me to resume I had been to the 'pancrack' and got another job, this time as a page-boy at a gentlemen's club. After about ten months I was told on the quiet by another member of the staff, 'Keep a look out for another job, Bill, as when you are sixteen you will require a wage rise so you will be replaced by a junior.'

Fortunately, it was about this time that my dad told me, 'There is a job for a bar-lad at the shed. If tha wants it, be at the office at nine sharp on Monday morning, but tha's not getting it wi my say so.' Needless to say I got the job.

1.   Bar-Lad

THE DATE was January 11th, 1934, and for the next 46 years of my life this was one of the most important dates to remember. This is because in the railway industry, particularly in the motive power department, seniority is vital. It controls when you do everything, until you either die or retire.

About the same time another lad joined the railway as a telephone lad and throughout our careers we developed a very strong friendship. But for a while there was doubt about his medical qualifications — he was an inch too short! The railway medical was and still is a very stiff one, particularly the eyesight test; at the drop of a hat it's off to the M.O. Poor old Frank, we practically stretched him that bit. We had him touching his toes every spare minute, we had him hanging from a bar over the sandhouse door and we took turns to swing by his legs. We put him through hell but he made it!

A bar-lad's job, as the name implies, involves attending to the firebars of locomotives. At times it was hard work. As fast as the engines came into the shed, they were barred, fired and oiled and off on their way again. A bar-lad's tools of his trade were a bar-rod (a steel rod about twelve feet long) and a paraffin flare lamp. The lamp had a handle so that you could place it in the firebox and thus see what you were doing, and then with the rod manipulate the fire-bars into place. Bar-lads worked as assistant to a steam-raiser, which experience-wise was invaluable as it provided practice with a firing shovel on an amazing variety of locomotives. Engines from other areas found their way on to the shed from time to time; one such was an 0-6-0 from Barrow-in-Furness which was not unlike a 'Derby 2' except that it actually had wooden brake blocks on the tender. It also carried a supply of spare blocks on the tender back as they were unobtainable anywhere else.

Another job a bar-lad had to do was cleaning fireboxes and brick arches when engines were washed out. I remember one lad who was sitting on the arch and cleaning the tube-ends when the boiler-washer in the smokebox accidentally put the wash-out pipe into a tube instead of the wash-out plug. The high pressure jet of water hit the bar-lad smack in the chest and he shot out of the firebox like a bullet, to the loud cheers of the fitters and all and sundry!

There was also much language from the bar-lad implying a serious doubt as to the parentage of the said boiler-washer!

The first shift of the week started on Sunday. You could smell the locos as you passed between them standing in rows waiting to be lit up. The only sound was a gentle hissing as the last drop of steam escaped. It is a sound and smell which lives with you; at the time it didn't mean much but now it is a nostalgic memory. Engines to be fired had first to be 'lined up' with coal leaving a small space in the middle like a bird's nest. The steam-raiser would then put in a shovelful of fire or lighter; it took up to eight hours to get steam up from the cold. Before lighting the fire it was vital to check the boiler for water. If the engine had had a wash-out, it was also essential to check the regulator, as sometimes it could have been left open to facilitate the filling of the boiler. It was not unknown for an engine slowly to creep into the turntable well as the steam built up.

One day, after I had been at the shed for only a short while, I was walking past an engine. The driver and fireman were washing their hands in the tool bucket; the driver looked down and seeing me, a stranger, said, 'Oy! What's name of thy job kid?'

Being still fresh from the gentleman's club and full of good manners, I replied, 'I beg your pardon, sir.'

The look of utter astonishment! His jaw dropped and the soap fell out of his hand. His mate looked at him and said sympathetically, 'Ee means, tha wat!'

The probationary period taught me quite a lot, in particular first-aid.

'Now lad, does tha know owt abaht first-aid?'

'No.'

'Then tha joins t' ambulance class, coss tha gets an extra pass for it as well!'

So encouraged by this grand old fitter and one or two other blokes, I started in the first-aid class and eventually joined a first-aid team. We made quite a name for ourselves in railway competitions. The fitter who took me under his wing was one of the many interesting characters I encountered during my railway career. He had more actual experience in first-aid than anyone I have ever known, and as a fitter he was second to none. If at lunchtime he was working at his bench, he would put down the hammer or whatever and simply wipe his hands on a cloth (not a particularly clean one), then tear a newspaper to hold between his fingers and carry on with his sandwiches. He ran a beautiful motor-bike with the old sit-up and beg type handlebars.

Another thing I learned about this time was that if you were given anything to do by a gaffer, you did it without answering back. If however you thought it was wrong, or not your job, you complained afterwards. The maxim was 'Do it now and complain later'. In fact right up to my retiring after 46 years, I still told my fireman or second man, 'There is only one opinion on this loco, mine and the wrong 'un!' It carries little weight however these days.

The next step up the ladder was to cleaner which in my case meant being transferred to Farnley Junction. On the railway it was accepted that workers were transferred to wherever the work was, and as it meant promotion you moved! 'Cleaner' meant basically cleaning engines, but in reality it was general labourer, and when not actually cleaning we were labouring on the ash-pit or sandhouse, shed-sweeping, assisting the fitters, calling-up and acting as messengers. These were but a few of the jobs we were called upon to do, and as demarcation was never heard of as far as we were concerned, we did as we were told. The job at this stage was never boring and it was the preparatory period for our next step, 'passed cleaner'—passed to act as fireman when required. So it was essential that we studied the rule-book which was the 'bible' and was thrown at us at every verse end. We had to pass exams on it to become firemen and drivers, and as we progressed through our career it became more and more obvious how important the rules were, especially those relating to safety and the protection of trains, particularly in unusual and adverse weather conditions.

One of the jobs we were given at Farnley was to meet trains at Farnley Junction and collect anything sent urgently for the shed. One day the chargeman cleaner shouted, 'Oi! You three, get down to the warehouse, there's three barrers to fetch.'

'Empty?'

'Course they are, unless tha can fill 'em!'

We went for them. Now those barrows were big, heavy, one-wheelers, very strong. The route back to the shed was quite a long one, so after a conflab we decided to go up the line. This entailed crossing a big junction, but as it was getting near home time we set off. We were just leaving when Frank shouted, 'Bill, how about this?' 'This' was a large heap of fresh horse manure. Grand, too good to miss, there is no point wheeling empty barrows when you can fill them, and we did. It was alright on the level, but when we were bumping over the junction the obvious happened and we lost some off. Again an opportunity not to be missed; we made small piles here and there and, after making horseshoe marks, the picture was complete. We often thought of what the platelayers must have said when they got to work next day and saw traces of horses in the middle of a busy junction miles away from the nearest field! We arrived back at the shed after the staff had gone home, so as our final act of devilment we jammed a barrow in the doors of the foreman cleaner and the leading fitter, and also the shed staff doorway, rather tightly and complete with fresh-smelling load! Needless to say we kept a low profile for the next day or two.

After about six months at Farnley we were made surplus to requirements—in other words redundant—so true to form the company decided in its wisdom that there was a greater need for our services at Mirfield, about six miles further up the road. We were not given any option, we were sent—it was move or else!

Farnley was an ex London & North Western depot and Mirfield was a former Lancashire & Yorkshire shed, so we were gaining experience on a different set of locomotives. At Farnley the bulk of the engines were 'Super Ds'. These were very powerful freight 0-8-0s but were extremely awkward to work on. To begin with, the firehole door was operated with a ratchet handle; to open, it had to be yanked down to swing the heavy round cast-iron door inwards and up. That was also the way the coal had to go to reach the front of the box. Now if that wasn't enough, there was no room to swing the shovel without making a large circle with your back hand to pass between the wheels of the hand-brake and the scoop—any misjudgement and there was no skin on your knuckles. The footplate sloped somewhat to the boiler; add to this the driver's and the fireman's stand were raised about a foot, so in effect you stood in a hole when you were firing. Like most other engines except those on the Midland, the 'Super Ds' were left-handed to fire, and as most people are right-handed it was an asset to be able to fire them as they were intended. It behove all cleaners on the shed to get plenty of practice. Driving these jokers was just as awkward as the regulator worked the reverse way to any other type. One of the best 'Wessie' engines was the 4-6-0 'Claughton'. It and the 'Prince of Wales' were also the most comfortable; it was like a ballroom on the footplate, but the handrails were a bit near together and anyone with a bit of a belly—a common feature among drivers—had to lift it over as they got on!

Mirfield on the other hand handled more local passengers and freight. The passenger work was done with the good old 'Lanky' 0-6-2 tanks, quite good little work-horses but at times a bit finicky at steaming and using quite a bit of water. They had Joy valve gear, which in action looked like a couple of knees and elbows swinging about. One 'Lanky' engine I was not keen on was the 0-8-0 'Teddy Bear'. It looked top heavy, the boiler was huge and as wide as the foot-plate. On the footplate the seats were just half circular pieces of wood attached to the cab side; there were no windows low enough to see out when sat down so it meant leaning back and looking round the cab side —a very awkward move.

At Mirfield as anywhere else, we cleaners were lumbered with jobs no other blokes wanted, and this time I think we hit an all-time low. In the yard was a row of railway cottages, about eight in number. Each had a dry toilet and as the yard was private land and considered dangerous to non-railwaymen this meant they had to be emptied weekly by—guess who? We three cleaners had to empty each one into three large cans and carry them across the yard and up some steps to the road where the corporation tanker would be waiting. The comments from all and sundry can be imagined.

9

2.   Fireman

IT WAS not long before we were again made redundant and returned to our own depots, and within three months were given an exam by a locomotive inspector and passed to act as firemen. Our rank was now 'passed cleaner'; this was 1936. As a junior my firing turns were confined to 'shed and shunt' for six months; these were conditions laid down by the local committee. It was important to get a firing turn as the pay for cleaning was 36s but firing was 57s per week.

My first firing turn was on a most odd type of tank, a 'Harry Lauder' 0-6-2 with a steam reverse which was practically unknown in our area. These engines had outlived their usefulness in their own area and had been sent to end their lives on the shunts of Stourton. They arrived complete with the necessary spares, although one item — a huge wooden pinch-bar — was not as supplied by the maker. We were not long in finding its purpose, which was to prise over the reversing link when it stuck in the wrong gear — an all too common occurrence.

Work in large sidings was never dull. Stourton had a sizeable yard with shunts at both ends and also very busy mineral sidings. It handled the southbound up traffic, the down traffic being dealt with at the adjoining Hunslet sidings which were equally substantial in extent. There were four other yards in Leeds and so there was quite a bit of inter-sidings traffic, with hindsight much of it probably unnecessary.

Each of the goods yards was under constant supervision by traffic inspectors and, especially during the weeks prior to Christmas, by the railway police. In those days beer and spirits came by train in large barrels. The beer train from Burton on Trent was well known, and many a wagon has been shunted into a road with a little more speed than was really necessary. One did not ask silly questions about the 'legs' under a particular wagon — 'snap time' was an enjoyable one in consequence. Spirits were another matter; if a leak occurred on a cask of spirit it could be detected at a considerable distance and the police were on the spot in no time at all. The police sergeant was a great bloke but was very keen and when he caught anyone it meant a rough handling, frightening a chap to death and then giving him a warning as to his future conduct. Sometimes raids were carried out by outside gangs; this was a different kettle of fish as it also involved the city police.

Hunslet was a typical rough working-class area with back-to-back houses and a large amount of unemployment. It was a common sight at street ends to see gangs of youths gambling, but muggings and rapings were practically unknown and with any rough-house brawls it was a case of a good thumping but never the boot. Burglaries were however commonplace but were usually confined to the big stores like the Co-op and involved foodstuffs that could easily be shared out or flogged. Saturday night was the customary time for the operation and any house in the district could get a knock on the door. As you opened it, a side of bacon, a sack of sugar or a half keg of butter would be thrust at you and the caller would immediately scarper. Sometime on the Sunday afternoon a complete stranger would arrive, dressed in his suit because in those days everyone put on their 'Sunday best'. There was no explanation, but before he left with 'the swag' he would 'whack' a portion off for looking after it. I have never known anyone refuse to accept or take part—in fact the majority were grateful.

It was at this period that the rule book took on a more important role, particularly as regards the 'calling-up area'. This was the area in which locomotive men were required to live as per the rules; it was arrived at by drawing on a street map a circle of one-mile radius from the depot. As this might not always be practical, a further extension was created by drawing another circle a further half mile out which was the 'advising area'. Men in the calling-up area would be called exactly one hour before booking time if their hours of duty fell between 10.0 p.m. and 6.0 a.m. In the advising area men would only be alerted if their turns were altered, for instance firing instead of cleaning or driving instead of firing.

The caller-up was usually a labourer. He got round on a company bike and on the whole was very punctual. He would knock until you answered, and would then call out the time and job and the state of the weather. 'It's 3.40, you're on at 4.40 for Skipton and it's raining.' At this stage you gave a knock back to indicate your acceptance. We lived in a back-to-back and, as the caller-up used to knock on the brickwork at the side of the door, the result was that the neighbours two doors on each side knew that Bill Addy was on at 4.40 and it was raining! They were not very amused, the more so because my father was also a driver on the other shift!

There was also a lighter side. A policeman, new on the beat, seeing a bloke hanging about at a street end for twenty minutes or so, got suspicious and crept up on the poor caller-up, 'Now what's yer game?' Another hazard was stray dogs, particularly the big ones left out curled up on the step. Some callers have been scared stiff, and many an engineman has missed a job because the caller-up would take no chances. It was however accepted practice that if the caller-up did not call you did not go and no action would be taken against you. Some old drivers who had opted for shunting work, for personal reasons, nerves or illness, would often tell the caller-up, 'When you call me don't shout for shunt, say London or Carlisle for the benefit of the neighbours.'

On one occasion, due to having to live within call, a number of passed cleaners lodged in a large house near the shed. The caller-up went to call one and, on receiving an answering knock, he shouted, 'Green on at 5.0 for Derby.' There was a knock back so he went on his way. Green never turned up; it transpired that it was Jones who had answered the call as they had all been out the previous night. Still a bit muddled he had muttered, 'Thank goodness it's not for me', and got back into bed without waking his mate. Needless to say Green missed a day's pay, and didn't he have something to say to his buddy.

In the period before the war things were a bit tight financially, so it was accepted that chaps who didn't have far to go home would sometimes take a small cob of coal 'to light the fire'. One morning a driver was on his way with the customary cob between his jacket and coat, his hand in the pocket supporting it. About five minutes from home the local bobby met him, 'Hello, Alf, just finished?' We all knew that the bobby liked a chat at that time of the morning, 4.0 a.m., and Alf knew that if he was caught with the coal he could well be prosecuted. He began sweating but the bobby chatted on for quite some time before saying, 'Well, Alf, you might as well potter off to bed lad, and I'll bet that cob is killing thee!' Then with a mischievous look in his eye he walked away. Alf was furious.

The locomotives at Stourton were mainly of Midland classes 2, 3 and 4. Classes 2 and 3 were good fireman's engines, it was just a matter of letting them see the shovel and they would steam. The class 4s were a bit more finicky; as they were superheated the blast on the fire was not the same as the class 3 so they had to be fired with a little more care. They were however good all-rounders and came in for quite a bit of passenger work, particularly on excursions to Morecambe.

We had one class 2 with only about three feet of cab top, No. 3451, and when the weather was rough it was most unpleasant. Another interesting type was a Kirtley class 2 which had all its springs — even those on the tender — above footplate level. There was another type at Stourton we called a 'Baby Austin', a class 7 0-8-0. These were very strong and small on the wheel, and at any speed would swing from side to side. Firing was an acrobatic performance, particularly as the space on the front was very limited, making them real knuckle grazers. They were numbered 9535 and 9537 to 9540.

As the bulk of the work at Stourton was shunts, 'trippers' and relief jobs, anyone who wanted to work on passenger and main-line trains had to move to other depots. There were various agreements which allowed this to happen. The nearest depot of that type to us was Holbeck which had quite a lot of attractive turns. Their passenger work covered the country from London (St. Pancras) and Bristol in the south to Carlisle and Glasgow in the north. There were few vacancies. The freight stretched from London to Carlisle, but there was plenty of rough work in disposing and preparing.

Shunt work entailed quite a bit of skill both for the driver and the shunter. In level sidings the shunter hooked the wagons off and signalled the driver to 'hit 'em up' until the speed was judged to be right, then reverse and repeat the process. If on the other hand there was a shunting bank, all that was required was for the shunt to draw the train up to the top and then ease the coupling when the shunter signalled. The sidings could have any number of roads from a dozen to about twenty, and there was a hand-signal by day and a hand-lamp signal by night for each road. The shunter would read the labels then put his pole on the buffer under the coupling, call the driver with a sweep of his arm, pass his hand between the buffers and chalk on the number of the next road before they came together. It was split-second timing — a mistake and he would lose his hand. It also involved a dedication to the job that earned him nothing except an extra 'fiver' (rest).

A shunter's job was and still is a hard one and bred some tough blokes. With an eight-hour day outside in all weathers all-the-year-round, they had to be tough and by and large they were a grand set of blokes with a great sense of humour to match. The shunters could take promotion to guards if they wished, according to vacancies, and a guard recruited from the sidings was a good one who could weigh a train to the last pair of wheels. He could also be relied upon not to be bulldozed by the sidings' foreman into taking too many wagons. Shunters whose job it was to brake the wagons into the roads so that they did not rebound back and foul another road were called brakesmen; as such they were paid danger money of an extra sixpence a day.

As Stourton was a freight depot, the class of coal we were allocated was of a low grade. Holbeck on the other hand because of its 'mahogany' work had a very good class of hard steam coal. When we wanted our coal stage filling up, the shed shunt would go to the sidings and sort out the required number of wagons, and then hump them up on to the coal stage. I say sort out — the sorting was the best Holbeck from the rubbish for Stourton! When the coal was put on the stage, the shed-man's job was to take the wagon labels into the office for the records. Now on occasions it so happened the labels were late in being handed in, and by the time a mistake had been found by the office staff a couple of wagons had already been put up. 'I'm sorry mate, the wagons have been started on', so for a day or so Stourton main-line jobs had a drop of Holbeck coal! After Holbeck had installed a two-grade coaling hopper, Stourton men would 'by mistake' coal their engines with Grade 1 whenever an opportunity occurred, until one day we were rumbled and were then watched every time we took an engine on shed. But if we couldn't get the best coal, we generally managed to come away with a few good fire-irons on the tender top. After all they were made at Holbeck smiths' shop but try asking for anything for Stourton! One got the rejoinder, 'They don't need good tackle there!', so it was a case of 'the Lord helps them who help themselves'.

A depot like Stourton with a predominance of 'trippers' had a considerable amount of tender-first running. Until the war came with its black-out sheets there was no protection at all from adverse weather. Not only snow and rain but fog or smog could build up a thick coating on the eyelashes and it felt like hard stone in the eyes. We had a turn we referred to as the 'death-trap job': Stourton to Keighley, back to Hunslet, to Keighley, then to Stourton, loaded each trip. At Keighley there were no facilities to turn so it was two trips tender-first. After one trip in winter, an old driver I was with had a lovely snow-white tache and bushy eyebrows covered in ice and hoar-frost — Frankenstein was bonny to him! Apart from the weather, the coal dust was a big hazard. In the absence of any protection from the railway company, I eventually brought my motor-cycle goggles into use.

Stourton Loco, having a fair amount of spare land, utilised it by storing coal. The stacks were large and well-built, containing amounts from 800 to 1,000 tons of top-quality steam coal. There were usually four stacks, built-up by passed cleaners shovelling from wagons. As an inducement, the arrangement was one wagon/one man which constituted an eight-hour shift. The first part was easy, but as the stack grew it got more difficult as the wall had to be built safely and so it took longer to empty the wagons. A stack carried a notice stating the amount, the grade and the date it was put down; it was left no more than two years as after that the quality deteriorated. During coal shortages it was sometimes necessary to lift the coal in a hurry and the one man/one wagon system would then be brought in again. If there were plenty of large cobs the wagon was soon filled, but as the stack got low the work got rather heavy. With a little subterfuge we overcame the problem; an old barrow inverted and placed in the corner, or old sleepers and planks, and the level soon built up! However, it wasn't long before someone thought of weighing the wagons and we were rumbled. When coal was really short, volunteers were sought at weekends not only from our own depot but also from neighbouring sheds like Normanton and Royston.

Life as a passed cleaner was far from monotonous. Whatever job you were undertaking, be it clearing engines or working in the sand-house, shed or ash-pit, you were expected to do it without someone standing over you. It was always nice to have a 'fiver' and share a can of tea, keeping one eye open for the gaffer. 'Look out there's a hard-hat man' was the signal for a general stampede back to work.

14

A 'hard-hat man' was any supervisory official—for example, Shed Foreman, Loco Inspector or Sidings Inspector. The hard-hat was his bowler, or derby as they were called; the hat along with a long dark railway mackintosh was his badge of office supplied by the company. It was quite an accepted part of railway uniform, but I remember once returning to the shed on a corporation bus when my attention was drawn to a bit of tittering going on. I looked for the cause of the amusement—it was one of our foremen on his way to work. It was a very hot summer day, and there walking quite unaware of the amusement he was causing was a rather stout man like Oliver Hardy, wearing grey flannel trousers, a sportscoat and open-necked shirt. Over his arm was his railway mac and there perched on his head like a pea on a drum was his bowler!

We had a few comics at Stourton too. There were two men called Gresham and Craven who knew every trick in the book and a few more besides. They had a couple of bowlers in their lockers which they would don when they knew a card-school was in progress in some quiet spot on an engine in the shed or in the sand-house. The mere shadow of a hard-hat man was enough to strike panic and the gang would scatter in all directions! This trick was more effective on nights, as no-one could identify them from a distance and yet no-one would wait until they were near enough. They were 'P.B. firemen'—in other words, firemen put back to passed cleaners, a form of redundancy with a reduction in pay, so the clowning was an excusable outlet for depression and frustration.

Locomotive depots were generally run quite efficiently and economically. They had their own ambulance men from every branch of the service—fitters, labourers and locomen—who attended classes in their own time and who after passing their exams were allowed an extra free pass as remuneration. They also had their own firemen (for putting out fires as opposed to firing locomotives); they were trained on the premises and paid an annual retainer of £5 a year but thanks to a responsible staff were rarely called into action. Until the practice was discontinued in the interest of economy, a person who reported a fire was paid 2s 6d.

While I was shunting in the sidings alongside the loco yard one day, a signalman shouted, 'Oy Bill! Do you still get owt for reporting a fire?'

'No.'

'Right, we'll let it burn!'

The fire in question was on a wagon of ashes on the ash-pit which was being filled by a couple of old boys—two shovelfuls, then a chat leaning on their shovels. On the blind side, unknown to them, the hot ash had started to smoulder and the wind had whipped it up. It was just beginning to burn nicely. The panic of the shed staff added quite a bit to our and the siding staff's enjoyment, but as we expected it was short lived. It took but a couple of minutes to move the wagon to the water column and dowse it out, with little or no damage.

3.

On the Road

BEFORE leaving the shed, a locomotive has to be prepared. The duties of both driver and fireman are clearly defined. The oiling of the engine is the driver's responsibility, the lamps and sand equipment the fireman's. There is quite a bit of checking to do also, before leaving the shed, such as testing the water gauges and checking the fire to see if it is 'clean'. On a heavy job a clean fire is vital. The ash pan must be clear; in fact, there are many more things too, if one is to have a good trip.

At Stourton we had no coaling plant, so coal had to be man-handled in tubs of about ten hundredweight and this was tipped on as we came from the shed. The fireman had to assist the coalmen and, if it was a long trip, it meant stacking the tender and whilst on the top deck checking all the fire irons. It is not generally appreciated that when the coal covers the fire irons, a fireman has only the handles to identify them. On later engines the larger tenders had fire iron tunnels, so the fireman could tell the dart from the rake. The handles were round for the shovel, oval for the dart and triangulr for the rake. The rest of the tackle was a bucket and four spanners, a box of twelve detonators and two red flags, and of course the firing shovel. The tackle had to be collected and returned to the stores at the beginning of every trip. The stores 'window' where we slung the tackle in was covered with a sheet of heavy metal, which must have been really tough to withstand the hammer we gave it. Wherever we went or whichever shed be it Midland, Geordie (all L.N.E.R. sheds were Geordie to us) or Wessie, the stores windows were always covered with the same metal and made the same noise as we slung the buckets in.

When train crews booked on duty, the first thing that had to be done was to read any notices pertaining to the route, weather and any other information, such as extra stops and so on. Ten minutes were allowed for this. It was the only time that the foreman was able to confer with the drivers regarding anything particular to report, but it was always understood that no driver was given Form I (charge of misdemeanour) on booking on, only when booking off, so as not to cause his concentration to be diverted or his judgement impaired. Unless it was a serious charge it was doubtful if it would, but that was the rule. I remember one time a new lad in the office came out with

16

'A letter for you Driver', which turned out to be a Form I. That was it. The driver turned round and walked out. When the fireman enquired where his driver was, as they were now ten minutes late off the shed, it took some time to realise that this joker had taken advantage of the inexperience of the lad. Nevertheless, the driver got his day's pay.

After each trip, no matter whether it was a short one or a long one, the locomotive had to be 'disposed of' on the ash pit. This, like preparation, was a laid-down procedure by the driver and his mate, but as a general rule both got stuck in. The fire had to be dropped or 'cleaned', the smoke box emptied, the ash-pan raked out and the engine examined for any obvious repairs — brake-blocks, springs and any blows or leaks. The engine was then shedded and the shed-man took over.

My first few trips on shunts and relief work taught me quite a lot, particularly the safety side of things, and the right words for the signalling, 'dolly on', 'peg off', 'whoa' for stop. These were the terms in use, so we always used them so that response was immediate, particularly 'whoa'. No-one makes any jokes about stopping or starting on an engine. I learned another thing, safety at work, the hard way. I was told that no railwayman should ever walk between two standing vehicles, if they were less than one wagon-length apart, without a look-out; failing that, the procedure was to duck down below the buffer height.

One afternoon, we had been relieved of a shunt in the sidings and were threading our way through the roads when the fireman who had taken over shouted out, 'Oi, Bill, has tha left this?' 'This' was my 'snap' bag so automatically I shot back, but as I got to the last road I was about to pass between the wagons which were about six feet apart when I heard a slight sound. At the same time, my mate gave a half strangled shout. I stopped in my tracks and at the same moment the buffers came together, inches away from my chest, with a loud bang! I could feel the cold air in my face from between them. The chap with my bag in front of me was as white as a sheet. He threw my bag to me and went back without another word. I think he was in more shock than I was.

About three-quarters of the work at Stourton was shunts and 'trippers' between the various collieries and had quite a good working with about ten or more collieries and had quite a good working relationship between loco guards and colliery shunters. Other sheds in the area also dealt with the same sidings and, as it was a regular trip, we knew which shed they were from and so the job worked quite smoothly. As trips passed each other on the road, it was the usual practice to acknowledge each other with a wave of the hand or a touch of the whistle, but in certain areas this was forbidden. There was one exception to the rule and this was when a passenger train ('mahogany') passed. As the crew were from Holbeck they would know us but would rarely acknowledge our wave. The amusing part was that the following day we would be together in the mess-room. I suppose the passenger trains gave them some feeling of superiority. It soon passed off.

A good sense of humour is the most precious of possessions and I have had, among my workmates, some born mickey-takers who never stick for a chance. One day I was standing in some sidings at the signal outlet, waiting for the passage of another trip. As it approached, my mate said, 'It will be Eric on this one', so we were ready as he came chugging up. But as it passed us, there was no-one on the footplate! The look of horror on the face of our guard who was on the footplate with us at the time! Knowing who was in charge on that particular job, I was not the least surprised. My driver, though, was not at all comfortable and was evidently in doubt. Later I was with Eric. He told me that they were on the framing, on the off-side, completely hidden from the near-side, but what they didn't realise, until they got back on the footplate, was that they had passed a signal box too. The signalman, seeing the apparently crewless train, practically had a fit. Not knowing the clowns who were on, he sent the signal to his mate in the next box, Waterloo Sidings, 'Train running away on right line'. This bloke could not be sure, but he carried out the correct procedure, setting the points for the goods line, to which the train was going anyway, but kept the signal on. To his surprise, the train slowed down and when the signal was lowered it carried on in the correct manner. As it passed the signalman hung out of the box to see what was going on and there was Eric with his mate, sat down and smoking his pipe at peace with the world. They gave a friendly wave as they passed. I would like to have heard the comments of the Waterloo signalman to his mate at Woodlesford box, 'You must have been drunk or daft or both!'

This period on the railways was completely different to modern times. Sections were much shorter and covered about a mile or so. Each section had a signal box. Signalmen, or 'Bobbies' as we referred to them, used to stand at the frame with their arms outstretched over it, one hand clearing to the box in the rear, the other sending the train to the box ahead whilst at the same time watching it passing. A signalman's duty was to note everything—correct headlamp code, no tail-lamp between tender and wagons, all wagon doors and catches correct and goodsbrake side lamps and tail-lamp intact. If any of these items were incorrect, then he sent the code to the box in advance of the train to 'stop and examine'. Signalmen were in constant touch with 'Control', so passing times were reported to them, and it was control who issued the 'please explain' if negligence or something similar was the cause. When for no apparent reason a signal was at red, both the driver and fireman would ask themselves, firstly, 'Have I got wrong headlamps on?' or, secondly, 'Have I got a headlamp on the tender end?' On the few occasions I left the headlamp on, it took only a minute, when the train slowed down, for the fireman to drop down the opposite side to the signal box and whip the lamp off and get back on the engine. When the signalman stopped us with 'You've a lamp on', we used to look blank at him, and with a 'Who 'as?' show him the lamp on the footplate. 'It's my mate. He's going off his rocker or something!'

So it went on, never two days, weeks or jobs the same. In fact, no two locos, even of the same class, were identical in performance. Some engines would have no difficulty in steaming. They would blow off just by showing them the shovel, but others of the same class would need coaxing to keep steam — 'a cold 'un'. Word soon got around when there was 'a cold 'un' on the shed, and if it was on a big job the fireman took steps to see that he didn't have the same problems as the last bloke. There were various things he could do and a lot of blokes resorted to the 'Jimmy'. This was basically a device to split the blast across the blast pipe, a rod shoved into a tube end and secured. There were quite a few ingenious inventions, the most popular being a 'Brummigem'. Designed by a chap at Saltley, it consisted of a blade across the blastpipe, secured by a circular clip under the jet ring and fastened with wing-nuts. It was easy to fit and remove and also fitted the lid of a lodging box. These devices were frowned upon by the management, but why I'm not sure. Some of the 5Xs and 'Scots' had a built in protrusion at the front and back, just inside the blast pipe, which to me looked very much like a suggestion of a 'Jimmy'.

The bulk of the main line work at Stourton was to the industrial Midlands. Lodging jobs took one to Derby and Toton, with Sheffield and Chesterfield being very congested areas. At times it could be an eight hour job just getting to Masborough and back home. The black spots where delay mostly occurred were the large marshalling yards, in our case Carleton and Masborough. Going north was not quite as bad, but Carlisle, with its numerous different railways converging was sometimes a problem. The principal cause of the delay, or block as we referred to it, was the practice of each marshalling yard to take in each train and shunt it. The result was that when we picked up our train again, it was only a wagon or two different to the train we brought! However, the figure of wagons shunted in their books was increased by the number of wagons passing through. Unfortunately this procedure takes time and is a very expensive way of running a railway. Sadly we have now gone to the opposite extreme in the interests of strict economy and closed the lifeline down. The only way to run a goods service is by having goods yards where they are required by the customer and where goods can be dispatched by the shortest route. The present system was bound to fail as any practical railwayman could see.

To be in a queue of two or three trains moving slowly to a signal and then sitting with your eyes glued to it, all the time keeping the fire just right and not letting the boiler get too low, did get to be a bit of a strain sometimes, but during the hours of darkness, 3.0 a.m. and 4.0 a.m. . . . . Well! That 'necessity is the mother of invention' was never more true. First, if there was a cold wind blowing from the tender end, no matter how you tried, you were frozen, so we baled out into the goods brake in front of us and had a brew with the guard. The guards, on the whole, were a friendly lot, so it was a case of 'There's my top-coat there, mate, make thissen comfortable and get down, lad', which we did. But on one trip we did this and dozed off, to be awoken by the rumbling that told us we were on our way.

'Hey up. Where are we?'

'Thars alreight, mate. We aren't at Masboro' yet.'

'Masboro' be buggered. We are on that train behind!'

'That' train was now about half a mile behind and it meant a quick dash along the rough ballast, nearly breaking our necks in the dark.

Another trick we adopted was to lean on the train in front, closing the couplings, so that when the train moved the noise of the tightening coupling gave us the tip. If we wanted to close our eyes we required something more positive, so we used a piece of sheet string to tie the couplings together. As the train in front drew away from us the coupling would lift up horizontally, the string would break and the thump of the falling coupling was enough to rouse us.

But these tricks could not apply when standing at a signal. The signalling was by semaphore-type, using a long arm with balance weight. So, we emptied our tool bucket, hung it on the weight and when the signal came off, the racket of the bucket was enough!

After arriving at the relief point, Masborough or Chesterfield or wherever, the first job was to get to the relief cabin. Now there was a place to write a story about! They varied from derelict salt stores, complete with a family of rats, to a discontinued lamp-room on a station. Some were ex-platelayers' cabins after the previous occupants had been moved to cleaner and healthier places. At Cudworth the relief cabin was a wooden hut with a split stable-type door. The heating was usually a stove, using coal that had dropped off locos. There was usually a gas-stove too, for tea mashing, and in the better equipped ones there was a cooker. The seating was long wooden forms and there were a couple of small tables and, to complete the fittings, a railway phone. This was a circuit phone with a form of code similar to morse code. For instance, the control could be contacted on all of them with one short ring, on a red button. The black button was for general use. On the circuit would be all the places that one would be likely to want—the signal box, the sidings, shunters and sidings inspectors. In fact there could be about seven or eight phones with their codes on a list, but, as you rang any particular one, each phone rang simultaneously and when you heard the call sign for your cabin the nearest man answered and relayed the message.

After being relieved and waiting for a service home, there was thus no rest, and if, as sometimes happened, the only seat was a couple of feet from the phone, you were up and down like a cork in a bottle. When a short ring went, it was obviously a call to Control and anyone could just pick up the receiver and indulge in a bit of ear-wigging.

Time spent in a relief cabin was rarely dull, and it was places like these that I met some of the best story tellers (tall ones) and the cleverest cheats at cards. I never played, just watched and listened. It really was one of the most entertaining ways of spending time waiting for your train. Apart from the stories, it was an education to listen to the many and varied dialects. There was Scouse, Geordie and Cockney, and one that never failed to be entertaining was broad Yorkshire, spoken naturally.

I think I can honestly say I have friends through the length and breadth of the country, from London, Grantham, Doncaster, Manchester and Liverpool to Carlisle, Carnforth and Skipton, thanks to my time on the railway. Whilst it has not made me wealthy, it has made me very rich in the knowledge that the pleasure and happy times I have experienced have been shared with so many and varied people.

Getting home after relief often meant travelling in a goods brake, and that was quite an experience, especially in the dark and on a cold morning. A brake will hold about ten men. There is a grand little stove in the middle of the floor, not to mention all the gear, guard's bags, tea cans, etc. In you get and fumble your way, trying to find a place to sit. 'Mind my bag mate!', 'Oi, that's my can thars kicked ower!' Eventually you get a kip, then when you get used to the dark you can spread your legs. The stove has been stoked up and is glowing a dull red about a foot up the stove pipe, hot enough to blister the enamel off the can if it's too near. After about half an hour you get used to the heat. If not you can always ride outside on the back veranda, but a hardened railwayman can stand any amount of heat. What does take a little longer to get used to is the smell of sweaty bodies, particularly after a heavy shower.

When, due to increased traffic, a train had to be strengthened, it was double headed by another locomotive. Where possible the assisting engine had to be compatible with the brake and it was arranged to have the smaller one at the front for obvious reasons. If both were fitted with vacuum brakes, then the driver of the leading engine could work the brakes on both locomotives. This did not excuse the driver on the rear engine from observing signals. He too could work both brakes if the need arose.

The trains which most frequently required double heading from Stourton were those from Carleton. These were mineral trains and usually of about sixty wagons, sixteen and twenty tonners. The guard always had a word with the drivers, not just to tell them the loading but to co-ordinate working. The route to Carnforth from Settle Junction was rather tricky with a loose-coupled train of that length. From Eldroth to Clapham the train stretched over about six gradients, so it was vital that all the crews knew what was happening at each end.

A driver who signs his route card for a particular route states that he knows each signal, junction and gradient and is able to work a train over the road in all weathers and conditions. This knowledge was never more important than on this road with these trains. As soon as we passed through the cutting at the top of Giggleswick Bank, which in spring was a beautiful mass of primroses, we began to pick up speed, both engines belting in, the 'baby oranges' flying from both chimney tops. The guard screwed his brake on and we kept this up till the last bridge. The train engine gave a little pop on his whistle as he shut off, then both firemen jumped to the hand brake and screwed it on hard. The hand brakes were left on until we got the distant at Wennington, then came the tricky bit. Some drivers let the train run out, others picked it up and drove. From Clapham, down the lovely valley past the silk mills at Bentham, it was a beautiful run. Returning in the dark, as we usually did, we found a new beauty. I was leaning over the side, attending to the injector and I couldn't believe my eyes, the 'six foot' was covered completely with not hundreds but thousands of tiny lights. I dashed to my mates' side to see if there were any there, but no. 'Come over here mate, and have a decco at this lot!' My mate came. 'They are glow-worms,' he said. But although I have seen them on several trips since, I will never forget that time. I encountered glow-worms again on the Derby road at Clay Cross, but where the Bentham ones were blue-white, those at Clay Cross were yellow-white.

On one trip to Carnforth I had just put the shovel down and was tidying up. We were passing Borwick and it was just breaking daylight, when suddenly, from nowhere, swooped a big beautiful barn-owl. It seemed to be coming into the cab and levelled out about six feet away from us. It was so close that I could study every detail. It was a straight line from wing-tip to wing-tip and kept with us for quite some distance, flying lazily over bridges as we passed under, joining us at the other side. It was uncanny. My mate and I kept up a dialogue with it: 'Well you lovely flat-nozed geezer. What are you up to? Checking on our timing?'

Carnforth was a 'private lodge', a little cottage near the canal. The lady was a very nice, homely sort, but we were only there a few hours. The train from Leeds was the 12.42 a.m. so it was early when we booked off and had breakfast in the canteen. After a wash and freshen up, I was off. If I felt like a walk, I sometimes spent about four hours walking to Morecambe. I then came back on the 'bus and went to bed. Other times I would have a walk to the lovely country around Kellet and collect half a dozen rabbits from the farms—two a piece for myself, my driver and guard. Sometimes the rabbits, being fresh trapped, wanted gutting. I was the only one who knew how, so that was a job I had to do in the yard before I could go to bed.

I have many pleasant and happy memories of Carnforth. In the war Carnforth was chosen to be the location for a film 'A Brief Encounter' and this was filmed, almost entirely during the hours of darkness, on the station. An obvious special dispensation of black-out regulations was granted and the glow of the arc-lights could be seen as far away as Clapham. The surprising thing to us was why? At Carnforth was one of the biggest petrol and oil dumps imaginable on the main-line side. The Army dump came in for quite some stick from the locals, and the comments about 'those foreigners' from London can be imagined. They were described as 'Fifth Columnists' — 'Why do we have to blackout, but not them?'

The coal at Carnforth was very poor steam coal and soon clinkered up. The only chance of getting steam was if the fire bars were covered with a scattering of broken limestone. Occasionally, a wagon of good Yorkshire Steam Coal found its way on to the coal stage: 'What about a tub or two of Yorkshire mate?'

'Aye, but tha'll fill 'em thissen!' and this I did. I thought it was worth it. Steam engines could be very finicky, so it paid to be particular about details.

We also had a few jobs to Lancaster Green Ayre, and loaded back from Moss Sidings. Moss was really M.O.S. (Ministry of Supply, a wartime department) at Heysham overlooking the harbour. It was a grand sight to watch the midnight boat leave. We were due to depart at 12.30 a.m. and as the boat disappeared into the mist, we set off on our journey.

The Carnforth double-heading lasted for nearly two years and I got a good share. In fact for a while I was often called 'Carnforth Bill'. However, with the appearance on the scene of the Class 8s, the trains were no longer needing assistance so we lost our double-heading job. But it lasted long enough for one driver to bring quite a fair amount of rockery stone home on the engine, to build a lovely one, and then name his house Wharton Crag!

It was a nice, pleasant autumn afternoon and we were on a 'tripper' to Apperley Viaduct. There was a hay-making scene as we passed Calverley. In fact the day had started very well and we were at peace with the world. There was a gentle breeze blowing, we had a Class 2 Ivatt, and at Apperley station we stopped and the guard hooked the two vans off for the yard. We drew up over the points and slowly came to a stop. The boiler had just entered the tunnel of the road bridge as we stopped, then, without warning, came a blast of hot air from the partly opened firebox and before I could get to the blower, there came an ever-increasing roar and a sheet of smokeless fire came back at us. The heat was almost unbearable. I was standing at the same side as my driver and the roar was increasing all the time and the fire becoming greater. The paint on the cab roof began to blister and burn! I was slowly driven to the side. I was

23

looking for something to reach the controls, the firing shovel or fire-irons, but I couldn't reach through the fire, so I climbed off. My driver, in the meantime, was slowly pushing back to the window at his side, and then he too started to climb out; but it was too big a drop to the ballast so he just hung out. I picked up a platelayer's shovel and climbed back on the engine. The regulator on this type was a fore and aft movement, so I tried to hook the handle of the shovel round it and pulled. I got it partly open, but she would not move. The brake was on a bit too strong. I leaned forward again. My hands and face seemed to be drying up and burning. I took a swing at the brake handle, caught it and, as the brake came off, we moved through the bridge. The backdraught stopped instantly. I put the brake on, shut the regulator and then pulled my mate back in. Phew!! Everything was too hot to touch. The smell of burning was really overpowering and all the cab top and tender end was burned and blistered. I never realised what a really terrible sensation it can be, to be involved with a serious fire. It was all over in about eight minutes, but the experience will last for ever.

4. The Carlisle Road

THE Midland route to Carlisle via Settle is acknowledged to be the most scenic in the country. Indeed, there must be enough books already published to satisfy anyone's thirst for statistics. My knowledge is based on nothing more than actual experience, gained the hard way, sometimes very hard. The first trip I can remember was firing a 'Derby 3'. This was a good loco steam-wise, but the driver resented me being with him instead of his regular mate. The old drivers were afraid that passed cleaners might not be up to the job, and that they would have to take the shovel themselves which a lot of them had really lost the knack of handling. After leaving Hellifield, he grunted, 'Get some on kid', and stuck his head out to look for the distant at Settle Junction. As soon as it was sighted, the regulator was opened, and whoosh! you were off.

The gradient at Settle station is 1 in 100. Now on a road that is insignificant, unless you're riding a bike, but on the railway it is a heavy gradient. By the time you have got as far as Helwith Bridge you are down to a steady slog. You are passing through the lovely limestone area up to Ribblehead station with Ingleborough on the left. Penyghent we have just passed on the right, and in front, beyond the notorious viaduct, Whernside. This is one of the advantages of being on the footplate, you get the whole panoramic view and it is truly breathtaking, in spite of having been shovelling like a slave.

By this time my driver had realised that I was up to the job and could cope, he was beginning to speak just odd words like, 'Tha's not far off top nar.' If the tank was not too low we could elect to pick up water on the troughs at Garsdale, so into Blea Moor tunnel we plunged. The summit of the bank is about a third of the way in, so we were belting at it. Then as we got nearer the end, which comes at you fairly fast, we shot out like a cork out of a bottle. As you leave the tunnel, a quick glance to the left shows the small graveyard of the men killed during the construction of the tunnel.

But there was little time to gaze about on a loco if you intended to get a full tank on the troughs. We got cracking at a fair lick and the fireman got the chain off the scoop handle and got ready to wind it down. The driver watched for the marker: 'Right!' and down you wound. The trick was not to leave it in too long: 'Out!' But sometimes the weight of the water against the scoop made it very difficult to get it out and the tank flowed over washing the coal (and the shovel). An avalanche of black mud sloshed over the entire footplate, and of course the driver told you things about yourself that you never knew before.

The troughs at Garsdale were the only ones on the Carlisle road. Also there was a turntable. It is such a remote place, high in the mountains and there was a branch line to Hawes, so facilities to turn and water engines were provided. I don't think I can remember a time when there was no wind blowing there. It was the custom, as I have mentioned previously, that before starting out from the shed a driver and foreman had to read any relevant notice pertaining to their journey. Usually, 99 times out of 100, one would read, 'Gale blowing, Blea Moor, secure all sheets'.

Sometimes, if we were getting low on water, we would stop at Blea Moor and get it at the column. During really rough weather, all goods trains were turned inside by the signalman. Once in the loop a gang of platelayers walked down each side of the train, tying down sheets which had broken loose. In fact, as we passed over Ribblehead viaduct, these very heavy tarpaulin sheets could blow off and sail away like dead leaves. Also, in a high wind, a platelayer would climb on to the tender top to help the fireman hold the water bag in.

On my first trip, I was sweeping the footplate as we ran on to Dent Head viaduct. The wind was driving down the valley and hit us sideways. It caught me completely unawares and blew me suddenly across, and only the tender handrail saved me from being blown off. The driver had his head stuck out, looking for the distant for Dent. I was more frightened than hurt but I had a sore rib and hip for a day or two. I told my mate. He grunted, 'Aye, it's a bit windy there as a rule.' I have thought since, would he have carried on without me?

At Ais Gill the road drops abruptly down to Appleby and, approaching, it looks almost like a roller coaster, it is as sudden as that. The scenery on this side is every bit as breathtaking as the other side, but not quite as rugged. In the crevices it is not uncommon to find snow as late as May.

The Carlisle road was not referred to as 'The Long Drag' for nothing. It was a real test of men and loco. You soon found out if the engine was a 'cold 'un', or if you had not prepared it properly. It meant stopping to 'blow up', that is to fill the boiler and get her 'blowing off'. It took about fifteen minutes to do this and brought all other trains behind to a stop. There were six sections on the bank and you could be sure that there would be at least four trains behind, queuing up. When a passenger train was due, every train was shunted inside, out of his way. This was a grand opportunity either to clean your fire or get some coal down, or have your snap, in that order.

There was something else. The signalbox was an ideal place to go rabbiting (rabbits to eat, not chatting). It was also a good place for fresh eggs. A brew of tea was an automatic act when in the box. I always found these signalmen were a most interesting set of blokes and knew the country around them.

No matter how remote the sidings were, you could be sure a couple of youngsters would materialise from nowhere to 'cab it'. After a few minutes, warming themselves, 'Do you know where the road comes near the line, mate? Just past the signal?'

'Yes.'

'Well, if you push that cob of coal off my mum will be able to get it!'

I suppose traders were rare visitors in these areas. The platelayers, when they ran out of fuel, used to stand a bottle on a wall near their cabin, an invitation to let fly with a piece of coal, and kick a cob off too. Some of the things I and other firemen have done were downright dangerous, but being young it didn't seem so at the time. If it had got to the bosses I suppose we would have probably lost our jobs.

On our way back from Carlisle, after lodging, we were on the look-out at certain signalboxes for something to take home, such as rabbits and the like. When the signalman had any, he would hang them in pairs over the rail round the box so we could see them from a fair distance on approaching. The price was fixed as a rule, at 2s 6d a pair. The price rose with the cost of living, but always to an odd amount. The last price I paid was 4s 6d a couple. The shopping method was thus. On approaching a box which usually had rabbits, we would hang our heads out to see in good time. 'Right Bill!' Having first made sure that I had a good fire on, the driver would slow down. We daren't stop. I would jump off, then sprint (not easy on the ballast) to the box. Up the steps, with the exact money in my hand (there was no change!), slap it on the table, swing round and grab a couple of rabbits. Back down the steps and sprint after the train! After clambering aboard I would grab the shovel and try to make up the fire again. The driver had to make up the time as we worked to a point to point timing. All the while this was taking place the signalman did not want to know. He stood impassive with his hands on his instruments watching the train go by. He had to report the time the train passed his box to Control, so he did not see owt! As soon as you got your breath back, you examined your purchase. Two rabbits. If you were in luck they could be two big beauties, but they could just as likely be one big one and one miserable thing not large enough for anything but a drop of gravy, with a liver all specked with white patches. But this was a risk we took, beggers could not be choosers.

Working loose-coupled trains, particularly on long jobs like Carnforth and Carlisle, was always something to get the adrenalin going. Trouble was a common link with excitement for the fireman at least, as he didn't have to take the 'can' back. Setting off one cold and very frosty morning at about 4.30 a.m. from Leeds, we were booked to stop in the loop at Gargrave for water, and the guard was booked to examine the train. Finding a hot axlebox, it was arranged for us to 'put it off' in the sidings. We drew up the main line to the sidings and stopped. The train was 25 wagons of coal and the 'hot box' was about six from the brake. The guard hooked off and drew the train up and the signalman set the road for 'inside' (the loop). The guard was going to hook the wagon off and the gradient would take care of it; he would follow and apply the brake.

That was what was intended, but there were two things which were not considered. Firstly, the weather was very frosty which makes the cast-iron couplings brittle; the second was fate. The guard signalled for the driver to ease the coupling, but the driver, being a bit on the edgy side, gave a little too much steam, then applied the brake too hard. The obvious thing happened and there was a sharp 'twang'. I looked back and saw a shaft of moonlight shining through a space abour four wagons away from the engine and getting bigger. 'We've brock 'em!' I immediately jumped down and started to race along to apply the wagon brakes but they had too big a start on me. Then I went down on my backside on the ice on the sleeper ends. The guard was still waving a stop signal to us; then came a dull boom.

This was a situation where it was vital to know your rule-book and I ran down to see just what the position was. Boy! There were wagons piled up amongst coal and various toiletries from the goods shed. The toilet on the end of the platform was completely demolished, buried in the rubble. My next duty was to run back to the loco and get my red flags and detonators, then run towards the approaching traffic on the opposite line, noting as I passed that the signal was still showing a stop position. But I learned very early on in my career that a signal does not stop a train. It is the brake! If it should happen that, for a variety of reasons, the driver does not see the signal then the brake is not applied in time. This is why detonators have to be put down at prescribed distances. I was on my way to the half mile when I heard what sounded to me like a train approaching. I fixed three detonators, ten yards apart, and with my bike lamp I started running towards it, waving like a madman. (The rule book tells us that any light waved violently denotes danger.) After running until I was short of breath, I stopped and listened. The sound was nearer but not quite so like a train now. I looked over the wall and there was a fast moving stream, rushing through a little waterfall!

On another occasion on the Carlisle run, at a nice steady pace, the driver checked the train and overdid it. There was the twang! I looked back and saw the tell-tale light shining through the wagons about three back. 'Right mate! I'll go back.' With that I dropped off whilst the driver endeavoured to let the rear portion of the train catch up. As it did, I checked to see the damage and if it was possible to couple the wagon with the undamaged coupling. Then I dived under and out, back on the loco and away. It was funny listening to the Carriage and Wagon Examiner on arrival at Durran Hill, remonstrating with the guard about bringing damaged wagons from Leeds, and the actions of the guard on seeing the coupling which he knew was alright when he left Leeds.

There was one occasion when we broke loose about half way down the train and, as we were only about half a mile from the sidings, my driver said, 'Watch this mate!' He skilfully allowed the rear part of the train to push us gently into the sidings. In the lodging house, a short time later as the guard came in, 'Oi, You two clever so and so's. I'll have your guts for garters if you try owt like that again!'

On a return trip from Carlisle, one nice Sunday afternoon, we were on our last little bit and came through the bridge at Bingley with enough steam to keep the couplings tight. Then, into the short tunnel at the end of the platform. I sounded the whistle on entering and coming out I saw an old man walking slowly onto the line, on a footpath which crosses the main line. He had a walking stick in his hand and seemed to be making hard work of it. I was horror-struck! I jumped up and whistled loud and long. The old man stopped, as if listening. I could only assume that he was nearly deaf. He was between the lines now and we were approaching very fast. We were no more than a hundred yards from him. I jumped to my mate's side and pulled him from the window. If there was going to be anything unpleasant to see, I didn't intend him to see it and be upset. He was a young passed cleaner of about seventeen. As I got to the off side, I looked over. The old man must have jumped, but not completely clear. Our steps caught his raincoat, spun him round and threw him to the ground. Fortunately for him, he fell away from the train. That man was exceedingly fortunate that there was nothing coming in the other direction.

Returning from Carlisle, the bank starts at Appleby. The climb is similar and involves a distance of 11 miles to Ais Gill. In the days of semaphore signals, the summit distant was always referred to as 'The Star of Bethlehem' and, boy, have I been glad to see it on a number of occasions. After each firing, we stuck our heads out to see it getting nearer. It was very well sighted as were many signals — some could be seen as far as two miles away. Going down the bank it was a case of 'Let it go'. At the bottom it was quite a sight when we were stood on the Giggleswick branch to see a loose-coupled train come off. The guard's brake was really spectacular as the whole brake gear was glowing a dull red and the wheels and blocks were just like bright orange catherine wheels.

In the 1940s a few passenger engines were fitted with speedometers as an experiment. These were the '5Xs' and 'Baby Scots' with parallel boilers. The timings were then speeded up and half minutes were introduced. We had our own opinions about that! After a while it was noticed that the trains were losing time, particularly down the bank. That seemed an odd situation, so after a period of observation a conclusion was reached by the loco inspectors. One of the best practical men we had at Holbeck at that time was Inspector Bert Nunn. It appeared that the old timers had no idea of speed in miles per hour, so when they actually saw on the speedometers what speed they were doing, it was a case of 'I think we are going a bit too handy mate' and they started to rub the brake a bit here and there. So Bert Nunn decided that for the moment we should uncouple the speedos and see what happened. Sure enough the timing got back. It was a fact that the old drivers were marvellous at time-keeping, point to point. If it was reduced by the odd minute, they would grunt and out with their pocket watch. 'Awright mate. Get a bit on!' and they would do it. But tell them how fast in M.P.H. and they didn't want to know.

The winter of 1981/82 was exceptional and compared in severity with that of 1947, but on the Carlisle road severe conditions 'over the top' were the rule not the exception. Drifting was fairly common place and the snow plough at Hellifield loco shed was kept in readiness every winter and used. So was the plough at Holbeck, as a second plough.

My most memorable trip to Carlisle was in one of these winters. When we arrived at Hellifield, we were informed that the road over the top had been blocked for two days. The snow plough was just about through so we were allowed to proceed. At Dent we were to follow the snow plough section by section. The snow in some places was much higher than the footplate and at Ais Gill only the cross-trees of the telegraph poles were visible and the signal box was entered by digging down and through the window! There was no communication with the next signal box, so procedure was on a time basis. The plough was given a fifteen minute start and we were told the time that it had left and proceeded accordingly, preparing to stop at a moment's notice should we catch him up. Eventually, as we got lower down the mountain side, it was a little easier and the plough was put 'inside' for us to make our own way. It must have been quite a spectacle to see us belting downhill with full regulator, steam and smoke, sparks from the chimney and two large jets of snow from beneath the boiler belly. The brake stretchers on a 'Derby 4' were situated very low across the loco, wheel to wheel, and were operated with a central pull-rod. As the blocks were at the front of the wheels, the snow caught the stretcher, pushing the blocks on to the wheels and meaning that we had to work harder. The snow came up through the motions and out like a giant white moustache.

Arriving at Appleby, I went up into the signal box and there frightened the signalman to bits, I must have looked that rough. 'Where the hell are you from?' As far as he knew, the road was still completely blocked and no communication had been passed to him. We were the first train through for three days. Once we had opened the line, there was a steady stream of traffic behind, and about four hours later there were both up and down lines open, but—the return journey!!

After nine hours' rest we started our return trip. As we left the barracks at Durran Hill, our own chaps were just booking off and of course there were the usual comments from them, 'Keep out of our road.'

'Don't worry, we'll melt the snow for you!'

However, we arrived at Appleby in good order and then set off up the bank into the snow once more and sure enough the block started all over again. All the signalman could tell us was that someone was having a bit of bother on the top. At Garsdale we found that three trains had been backed 'inside'. We too were put in. The traffic inspector told us that the up road was blocked. It seemed that the snow had drifted badly and pushed a van off the road and as fast as the platelayers dug it out it filled up again. We were eventually relieved by the same men who had just booked off as we set off from Carlisle. They had had nine hours rest and were brought with the relief for the other crews in an engine and brake from Carlisle. We were eventually sent to Hellifield in a ballast brake and then caught a passenger train home. I had spent twenty-one hours on duty and in all that time all we had had was a few sandwiches and two cups of tea, but in those sorts of conditions food is not the priority. Getting home is the main worry.

5.

Wartime

DURING the 'Cold War' — the twelve months before the actual outbreak of war — I was firing in the local 'trip link' and the driver was telling me that he would like to be able to speak a foreign language. Well, I thought it was not a bad idea.

'Any particular one?'

'Well, I have some nice records of German operas, so it might be an ideal opportunity so I could enjoy them a bit more.'

So I bought some textbooks: 'Hugo's German Grammar in Six Months without a Master' — at least that was the claim. We stuck at it for about eight months and as we had quite a few shunts in the link, we had plenty of time for studying. But the war was imminent. Shunters and guards that got on the engine and heard us trying to converse in German gave us some very odd looks. We were actually accused of being fifth columnists, defeatists and so on. We eventually gave up the idea, not I hasten to add because of the feeling against us. I could stand that. I was amused really and played it up a bit. No, what beat us was our lack of knowledge and our own grammar, having both left school at fourteen. Really we were, and I perhaps still am, a bit lacking in that subject.

War broke out and the tension among some chaps was high. It only needed a joker like me to ask 'What are those black crosses on that plane for?' to send them stampeding to the air raid shelters. But as the war progressed we got accustomed to the distinctive sound of the German planes.

All locomotives were fitted with blackout sheets that had to be in position night and day at first. Also, half of the front window was painted with anti-gas paint, which was supposed to change colour in a gas attack but it got so dirty that it could have been impossible to notice any difference.

One nice hot summer day I was working a train to Carnforth. The blackout regulations had been relaxed to allow the side sheets to be left down during daylight, but my driver was undecided about this. 'We had better leave them up, just in case!' I fired that engine all the way in a tent! Needless to say, my mate had his head out practically all the way. I kept wishing he would have it knocked off! I must have lost a couple of stones in sweat.

Bill Addy (right) alongside a High Speed Train at Leeds station with Driver Nelson of Holbeck shed.

West Riding engine sheds. Above: Leeds Holbeck—a view well illustrating the atmosphere of a steam locomotive depot. Bill Addy transferred here in 1966 at the end of the steam era. (L & GRP) Below: Mirfield, where the author was a cleaner in the 1930s. The coaling stage is being passed by a freight double-headed by a 'Teddy Bear' and a 'Super D'—neither of which were popular among shed staff. (D. Ibbotson)

At Stourton shed Bill Addy frequently acted as fireman on class
4F 0-6-0s. Here a Stourton locomotive, No. 44028, pauses on
shunting duties near Holbeck station. (Eric Treacy)

North of Leeds. Above: Battling against the elements with an 0-6-0 on the Carlisle road could often be a gruelling experience. No. 44451 is leaving the refuge siding at Ais Gill with an up freight in relatively calm weather. (Derek Cross) **Below:** The author at one stage became known as 'Carnforth Bill' owing to the amount of time he spent firing double-headed freights from Leeds to Carnforth—one such train is seen here near Keighley. (Real Photographs)

After being passed for driving in 1945, Bill Addy transferred to Farnley shed where most of the passenger work was on trains from Leeds to Manchester and Liverpool. The 'Black Fives' were the preferred class on this steeply-graded route, putting up fine performances as captured in this view near Marsden. (Eric Treacy)

The diesel age. Above: The 'Deltics' were a favourite with enthusiasts but drivers initially found them both noisy and draughty. This study shows one in original two-tone livery passing Beeston Junction with a Leeds - London express. (Eric Treacy) Below: Some of Bill Addy's earliest experiences with diesels were on the 'Trans-Pennine' units, one of which is here shown in latterday guise at Leeds station. (A. Haigh)

In the 1960s the author initiated a series of talks to schoolchildren in order to get across the dangers of trespass and vandalism. These pictures show 'the message' being put over at Dewsbury (above) and York (below). (Dewsbury Reporter; British Rail)

Presentations—Receiving the British Empire Medal from John Silkin on October 23rd, 1974 (above); last day of railway service on March 8th, 1980 (below).

The railways, along with other big industries that worked on shifts, were given a prior air-raid warning system. Yellow was stand-by, purple was raid imminent. With the purple the lights were extinguished at a main cock which was installed specially. In the messroom one evening I was having my snap and suddenly the lights went out. 'Another ruddy raid!' someone muttered, and we sat waiting for the inevitable sirens which followed the purple. After about ten minutes there were no sirens or any other activity. The messroom bloke got his torch out. 'There is no raid! It's this valve. Someone must have leaned on it.' Stourton was still lit by gas and the large mains had a very greasy substance round the valves which needed little to turn them. The messroom chap turned the gas back on and we lit up and carried on as usual.

After we had finished our grub, my driver and I went into the shed to get our engine ready for our next job. I went to the stores for the tackle (shovel and bucket of spanners, etc). As I did so, I noticed all the windows were open. Strange! The stores blokes were not exactly open-air fiends. In fact, just the reverse. I would say they were more inclined to curl up with a top coat wrapped round them in front of a great roaring fire. I shouted the engine number out for the tackle. The stores bloke looked up at me and his eyes suddenly lit up rather strangley.

'Have you just come from the mess-room?'

'Yes', I said.

He almost screamed, 'George! I've found the bugger!!!! It's 'im! It's Bill Addy!'

I looked at him. I just couldn't work out what was the matter with him.

In came the foreman. 'Now then Bill! What's yer game?'

It appeared that when the gas was turned off in the messroom (the foreman's office and the stores were all on the same pipe) and the lights went out, they thought it was an air-raid warning. Normally the lights would automatically come back on when the warning was past but such was not the case this time. It was not until the place was full of gas that the mistake was discovered. There was a lot of choking and spluttering going on, with a lot of 'I'll kill the so-and-so that did this!', not in those exact words of course. Seeing me was like lighting the blue touchpaper. I was the likely bloke to do a thing like that and, believe me, they took a lot of convincing that it was an accident.

The signalmen at Dent and Garsdale, during the intensive bombing of Manchester and Merseyside, could look across from their high position and see the glow in the sky from the fires. Also, they could tell when an air-raid was imminent by the large number of planes which passed overhead. When we were stopped for any reason, these signalmen always seemed well up on the news. On enquiring, it turned out that one of the signalmen had a good radio set and always had it on. He also had it near the telephone, which he had off the cradle and so did all the other signalmen on the circuit! All six of them. The odd thing was, it was never short of power. All the boxes were gas or oil lit, but this radio was never low. Now, the telephones in the boxes were battery operated, and when all six were wanting renewing at the same time, and sooner than normal, the signal and telegraph engineers were a little suspicious to say the least. They made a thorough investigation and found that a signalman at Dent station was tapping an electric cable that was on a telegraph post just a couple of feet away behind the signalbox. Needless to say, he was sacked and also fined for stealing electricity.

All the excitement during my firing career was not confined to the Carlisle road. On one occasion I had been lodging at Toton (Long Eaton) and we were given the job of relieving a train from Corby. It was 4.30 a.m. and dark. The blackout was still in operation. Across we went to the train and I looked, in the dark, at the engine.

'Whats that?' I said.

My mate said, 'Don't worry, Bill, it's a Garratt.'

Well, up to that time I had only seen them in books. I had vaguely heard reference to them at Toton. They were largely used to work the heavy coal trains from Toton to Brent power station. We climbed aboard and the space on the front was great, just like the Midland 'Crabs'.

The fireman I was relieving said, ' 'as tha 'ed one afower mate?'

'No, mate', I said. 'I've never seen one afore!'

'O.K. This is the damper, the injectors are the same as the usual type, she blows off at 200, and that's the handbrake. Keep plenty of coil on and tha'll be alreight.'

With that remark, he left. That was my one and only bit of tuition on a Garratt.

The Garratts were a very powerful engine. They could take the limit in any length of train, loaded or empty, without overloading. They were really two locomotives in one — one boiler, but two sets of motion, two tanks and one coal bunker. The wheel arrangement was 2-6-6-2. There were two different tenders, the old type being cylindrical and 'welsh hat' shape. The idea was that, when the coal was getting back, the doors would shut and the steam be used to revolve the entire tender. It was successful to a degree, but at times it was known to jam with coal in the runners and then the engine was a casualty. So the later ones had a square type. These engines were very greedy and as soon as you had put one shovelful on you had to get the next one ready. The fireboxes were as wide as they were long and to aid combustion there was a row of holes, about the size of tennis balls, across at footplate level leading into the fire. To get a shovel of coal into the back corners was a work of art. I was given to understand that regular firemen on Garratts were issued with leather aprons as protection.

So we set off. Our train consisted of ninety wagons of 'monkey muck' (iron ore). These engines had a peculiar beat as there was no co-ordination between the two halves and they both exhausted through the same chimney—it was a 'whuffity whum' noise. It was a steady pull up to the top of Moreton Bank, with only a brief stop at Tibshelf for water, and as it began to get daylight I looked back at the train. Boy! It seemed miles to the guard's brake. In fact it was more or less completely out of sight most of the time. At the top of the bank we were on the main line and as we approached the top I had let the steam drop back a little to about 175 lbs and allowed the water to drop a bit to help keep her quiet. No blowing off!

I was sweeping the footplate as the driver shut off and we started down the bank. Out of my eye corner I saw the driver slowly apply the steam brake slightly to bring the train on to us, but there was no feel of it rubbing. He gave it a bit more, without any more effect. Judging by the position of the handle, we should have felt it rubbing hard, but we were still increasing speed! I jumped up and opened the damper then banged some coal on to get it blowing off, as the steam pressure is the pressure on the brake. I next grabbed the hand-brake and wound it on hard, but instead of biting hard it just rubbed too. By this time we had the brake full on, with only rubbing and little or no reduction in speed!

This is the moment when a feeling of helplessness and frustration comes over you. I don't think in my case it was fear, more 'what can I do next?' The driver then put on the sanders, I sounded the whistle, popping as a signal to the guard and the signalman, then we reversed the gear about half way. We passed the distant for Coney Green. It was on. This meant that we were most likely going down the goods line. As we passed the box the signalman was at the door. He evidently understood our predicament and we shouted, 'Tell the guard to swing on his brake!' Knowing that the goods line was usually occupied with trains being shunted at Clay Cross, at the bottom of the bank, I began to feel an odd sensation. Fear, I suppose. We were now in full reverse—the racket the engine was making!—and we were still popping the whistle. Now we had done all there was to do. I opened both of the doors: on a Garratt they were narrow and full steel ones, not easy to shift in a hurry. I had them both open as far as they would go, so my mate and I would have no difficulty. I had never been so near to jumping before.

Now, whether the signalman had signalled to Clay Cross that we were running away, I don't know. This was the first time in five or six years on the road that we had had a clear run through Clay Cross and as the gradient levelled out we were able to bring the train to a stand at Hasland, not far from the engine shed. We brought the fitters out to the brakes, who, contrary to regulations, scotched the wheels and adjusted the brakes where we were. I think that it was about half an hour later that I felt rather groggy and began to tremble. The driver made little comment about it, except to curse the Toton driver for not attending to his engine before starting his job. To my driver, it could have been just another ordinary trip.

There were very few things to laugh about during the blackout, but I remember one occasion. I had been visiting a relation at Halifax with my wife and her parents. We were in a non-corridor compartment and it was practically full. It was lit with one bulb in the centre. The bulb was painted with black paint and a small hole was scratched at the bottom, throwing a very poor light. The side windows were also painted out, except for half of the middle one. Add to this that the stations were blacked out the same, so it behove anyone travelling at night to know where they were and where they were going. On this particular trip we ran into Low Moor which had an island platform, both sides of which were up and down roads. As we ran in, the porter called the station and a young lady got up and came to the door where I was sitting and got hold of the handle. I hadn't noticed any lights as we ran in so I said, 'It's the other side, miss.'

She half smiled, 'No, I think it's this side.'

A soldier facing said, 'You're wrong love, it's the other side.'

She turned angrily to him, 'It *is* this side, I live here!', and turned the handle, put her shoulder to the door and stepped out! There was silence for what seemed about half a minute, then a 'scrunch' sound as ballast was disturbed, and a white face appeared at the floor level, 'It is the other side!'

I immediately jumped down onto the ballast beside her. At moments like these you realise just how high the running board is from the ballast. The problem was how to get the lady back up quickly. The soldier pulled as I shoved and with an embarrassed 'Thankyou' she scattered out of the other door. At the time it was not funny, but I've had quite a few chuckles since.

Another incident which occurred at Stourton Up Sidings illustrated the tension which existed with some blokes during the war. It was just after 10 p.m. when a guard, looking round his train, saw what he described as an 'unexploded bomb' to the sidings inspector.

'A what?' he said.

'Then come and see for thissen.'

With that the inspector, the guard and some shunters marched off to investigate. What they found was a bullet-shaped lump of iron, about a foot long and four inches in diameter. Obvious War Department material. There were strict instructions about W.D. stuff not under any circumstances being handled by anyone but Army personnel. It was obvious to most of us that it was really harmless but the order was carried out, 'Stop the road and the road each side.'

It so happened that the traffic on these roads was important stuff for Birmingham, Derby and London, so it was not long before a gaffer shot down. 'Now what the hell is going on here?'

The sidings inspector told him, 'We have an unidentified object down twelve.'

'Let me see!'

The inspector and 'Abie' went down the road. Suddenly a howl that could be heard all over the sidings told us they had found it. 'That damn thing! There are dozens laying about all over the sidings. They are solid iron. A plank has burst out of an old wagon and they are being picked up by the platelayers so get these roads open and the traffic moving.'

'Just a minute, that isn't quite all,' the inspector told him.

'Now what?'

'Well, I sent for the Bomb Disposal in accordance with the instructions and they should be here soon.'

'What! you have?' Abie practically burst a blood vessel. 'Carry on. I'll go and meet them.'

Where upon he picked up the object in question and marched off. He went down to the main road which passed by the sidings with 'it' under his arm. Normality resumed in the sidings.

After about twenty minutes, the Army suddenly appeared from nowhere, in full gear. 'Whose in charge! Where is this 'ere bomb thing?'

For a moment, silence. 'Oh, er, our inspector has it.'

'Where is he?' they demanded.

'He has gone looking for you!'

Well, for the second time that evening the peace was shattered. This time the air was blue and every other possible colour. It is questionable which language was the most descriptive, Army or war-time railway. Then followed a full search of the area — sidings, main line and the main road — but no Abie.

What actually happened was this. When Abie got down onto the main road, dressed in his long black railway mac and bowler, he stood near the road bridge which carried the main railway line. It was very dark. On the other side of the road was the entrance to the 'Bison' works, which had a security post, complete with a contingent of Home Guard. Having heard a sound of movement, they crept over to investigate. Seeing the dark figure, motionless, they challenged, 'Halt! Who goes there?' and shone a torch on him. Well, no amount of explaining would satisfy those keen blokes. As I have previously mentioned, the tension which existed was no joke. The result was that Abie was taken into custody, protesting, but it carried no weight with them. They said, 'We'll send for our officer', and the officer was contacted. 'Keep him there until I come,' he said. Well, this bloke had just gone to bed and nothing short of a full invasion would fetch him during the early hours. He eventually arrived to interrogate Abie at about 5.30 a.m., changing-shift time. Naturally, Abie was cleared by a few phone calls but a very sheepish traffic inspector had a very rough passage for quite some time after.

Apart from an occasional stick of bombs, Leeds came through the

45

war fairly lightly but there was one heavy raid. I was on at 4.0 a.m., the raid was over and it was just breaking daylight. I reported for duty but there were quite a few that missed. The foreman said, 'Bill, you go with Ernie to Holbeck station.' 'What are we going for, Ernie?' I said. It was to relieve Derby men on the fire brigade train. A bomb had made a hit on the station and as the civic authorities were busy with their own commitments, the railway had to look after its own. To the best of my knowledge there were only two purpose-built fire brigade trains in existence — the other was at Crewe. Both alas are no more.

Inevitably, war was a breeding-ground for nostalgia that is usually triggered off by a piece of music or song. It is also a fact that the older one gets, the more profound the feelings. One such occasion for me was an incident during the early part of the war. I was a fireman at the time and we had been relieved off a train at Hasland. It was just after midnight and there was nothing to work back so we had to make our own way home. Back to Chesterfield we walked. The last train had gone so we went into the blacked-out waiting room to catch any train — goods, parcels, anything. As we entered we disturbed some 'bodies' laid in the dark in various postures. The 'bodies' turned out to be five or six young soldiers. We mashed a couple of cans of tea and brought out the few biscuits we had left and shared out. As we chatted, I noticed they were all from a variety of different regiments. The two I was sitting with were from Wick in Scotland; the others were from as far apart as Cheshire and Lancashire. Then, as sometimes happens, someone started singing and one lad had a mouth-organ. We all joined in and it was great fun while it lasted. I then began to wonder, 'I say, mate, what train are you waiting for?'

'Nay laddie, we came by train. We are waiting for transport.'

The door opened and a couple of smart N.C.O.s came in. 'Are you lot from Hardwick?' And with a 'Cheerio! And thanks for the tea' they trouped out. They were volunteers for the parachute regiment. I have often wondered since, how many of those lads survived, if any. The song they sang was 'Jealousy'.

The Middleton railway is connected to B.R. through a spur into Hunslet Down sidings and up to and including the war years, quite a bit of mineral traffic was exchanged, but a lot of important traffic came from the Hunslet Engine Co. As far back as I can remember, new and prototype diesels were brought from their works in Jack Lane and taken on to the Middleton branch and left to work for about a week on test. Hunslet Engine Co. was situated in a very congested industrial area and locos had to cross a busy road. A Stourton driver had to conduct these locos from the works to the sidings. Leaving the works, a flagman had to stand in the road with a red flag to stop road vehicles, but no-one knew what to do when a lady on horse-back came trotting up. It is doubtful whether the old boy with the flag had ever seen such a splendid sight. He just gawped. Up came the tripper, a steam engine this time. The horse was certainly not used to them, so the inevitable happened. It shied, then shot off like a bat from hell.

About two days later, the driver was summoned to the office of the Gaffer at Leeds and there was the lady with him. She demanded and got an apology from the old driver. She was evidently a lady of means.

Any locoman who goes through forty-odd years on a job without being involved in some form of serious accident, such as a train smash or a suicide, is blessed with more than his ordinary share of good fortune and luck. I consider myself one of these. Accidents were more likely in the steam era but in these days of modern safeguards things are much better. I have had a couple of unpleasant occasions, however.

On Monday morning, 11th October, 1943, my father and his mate set off at 4.30 a.m. from Kirkstall for Carnforth. It was a little bit foggy, with visibility at about a hundred yards. It was a train of coal, but next to the engine was a cattle truck loaded with bales of straw. The locomotive was a 'Derby 3'. All went well until they arrived at Steeton, between Keighley and Skipton. 'Inside driver,' called out the signalman. My dad drew his train up over the points, the guard called him back and slowly he began to reverse into the sidings. The train was just four wagons short of being inside and the locomotive was opposite the signal box. The guard was at the bottom of the signal box steps when they heard the sound of an express approaching rather quickly and loudly. As they were on the down main line, my dad assumed that the express must be on the up line, so he called out to the guard, Sid Coupe, 'Look out Sid! Give this joker plenty of room!' But the express was the 2.47 a.m. from Leeds to Edinburgh, on the down and going full belt.

What happened next was told to me in detail by my father. At the moment of impact the goods locomotive was travelling slowly backwards towards the passenger engine, a 5XP, which then climbed the coal wagons and ran towards the goods engine. My father saw it coming towards him and was pushing himself into the corner of the cab as tightly as he could, thinking, 'Good Christ. He's on us!' The speed of the express drove the remainder of the goods train and loco about a hundred yards and the passenger engine climbed over the wagons and towered over the cab of the goods engine. In doing so, it ripped its ash-pan off the tender end. My dad found himself looking up into the actual fire of the 5XP. But providence was to hand. The cattle truck collapsed under the weight of the 5XP and the engine rolled sideways off. In doing so, it smashed its safety valves off on the platform edge, emitting a jet of boiling water and steam up the Kildwick road. No-one was killed, fortunately, but when my father eventually got to the signal box the guard thought he was seeing a ghost as the crash happened right in front of him—a matter of twenty-five feet away. He was really in a state of shock.

This was the stage at which the Americans entered the war arena. Their troops were entering this country via Stranraer and then south to Carlisle so there were quite a few specials for Stourton men. The guards in particular did well out of them. For instance, as they walked through the train, the Americans bombarded them with questions, like, 'Conductor, have you been in an air-raid yet?' or 'Have you heard a German bomb go off?', then would follow 'Can you explain how many of these make one of those?' 'These' and 'those' were the coinage. The guards usually finished up with a pocket full of loose change and several packets of Camel cigarettes.

One night, about this time, I was firing on a shunt at Hunslet Up Sidings. There had been a steady fall of snow and it was about six inches thick under foot. Then, along came a Compound on a special, roaring up the main line. It was obviously a troop-train, it couldn't be anything else at that time. I watched it approach with not a little interest. We had reason to: just a month earlier one of these 'Yankee' troop-trains, with a few 'snap happy' soldiers, had taken pot-shots from the train windows at some cows as they passed Thwaites, between Keighley and Bingley. Some of the cattle had been wounded but not too seriously.

I watched it go by. Just as it did so, as the engine approached Pepper Road bridge, there was a loud crack and a flash! It came from the engine wheels. My driver shot across to my side, 'What the hell was that?'

'I think it was a detonator, I'll go and have a look.'

The train had gone, but as I got to the spot, a shunter arrived there too. We looked and found that one of the two detonators had been 'cracked'. I went to the signal box at Hunslet South Junction, 'Have you a spare "det" for your home signal Arthur? That passenger train cracked one.'

Arthur was as white as a ghost. 'Bill, that passenger train has just run past all my signals.'

'Cor, he'll be for it then, won't he?' I said.

'Bill, there's a train standing at Wakefield road being relieved. He must have smashed into him!'

'God help us!' I said, as I shot off down the steps and started to run to the scene. Wakefield road was about 250 yards away.

As I started, Arthur shouted after me, 'If you need any first-aid tackle, let me know, we have plenty here.'

The scene at Wakefield road as I got there was that the troop-train was standing with its front coaches just through the bridge. There was a troop of soldiers carrying their gear, walking back from the leading end. I asked the officer, 'Anyone hurt?'

'We are O.K. chum, but there is someone at the front end that needs attention. I think he's in a bad way.'

I dived through the bridge, and what a sight! There was a heap of smashed wagons nearly as high as the bridge, with the Compound on top, laid over on its side. There were railwaymen all over. One was on the passenger engine, raking the fire out before the fire box collapsed and the boiler burst. A couple of blokes came up to me, 'Bill, thank goodness you're here. They want an ambulanceman in the relief cabin quick.'

I ran across. Inside, laid on a stretcher on the table was the guard. He was still in his railway overcoat. I asked him, 'Now my old flower, where does it hurt most?'

Without opening his eyes he said, 'Bill, it's my shoulder.' Someone stuffed a set of scissors in my hand. I had just got to his collar bone when the ambulance arrived, so I secured his arm, made him comfortable and then he was away to the Infirmary.

The Guard who had just been relieved was on the brake step at the time of impact and was thrown clear. He picked himself up, walked across to the shed, booked off and went home without speaking a word to anyone. He was in a state of shock. The name of the guard was Sid Coupe. He was eventually 'taken out of the brake' for his own protection. He had been involved in about five major accidents and come through without any physical injury. The law of averages said it could not last.

6.   Driving

I WAS passed for driving in July 1945. The exam was, and still is, quite a stiff one. The object of the exam is not to fail men but to ensure that they know their job thoroughly. When out on the road with a train—it does not matter whether it is empty wagons or children going on a trip to the seaside—the responsibility for its safety is the driver's and nobody elses. In certain cases of accidents there may be some contributory factors, but the movement and the stopping is done by one man, the driver. He must never allow familiarity to enter into his work and never take the job for granted. As soon as the engine leaves the shed, the driver is in sole charge of both loco and mate.

I've always enjoyed my job, in fact I feel privileged to have worked through the steam era and to have seen the changeover to diesel traction. I've had some of the finest mates, firemen or second-men as they are classed on diesels.

During the steam era, we did our schooling in our own time at Mutual Improvement Class. Also, as we were booked with a driver for long periods, twelve months at a time usually, he would give you what help he could, driving on certain jobs so that he could keep an eye on you. He would give you help on the faults and the rules, assuming he could remember his own exam. The exam took two days. The first day was devoted to rules and faults and failures. The second day was devoted to actually driving a goods train one way and a passenger back. During the test the fireman had to be told everything to do and not do anything until instructed by the driver.

Being passed for driving did not necessarily mean being a driver. It was the same situation as being a passed cleaner and the pay for driving was the same trip system—313 trips for a year's driving, which took two and sometimes more years to get. Having passed the exam, the next step was to take out a road card, an official and legal document which required a signature by each driver who worked that particular route. It was a declaration to say he was fully conversant with the position of *every* signal, gradient, curve, crossing, in fact everything. Also he had to know it in fog, snow and any other type of weather. Even if the signal failed and there was no light in it, it was still an offence to pass it at danger. Road learning was thus a very important business, the signing of a road being verified every six months by a senior foreman.

At a small depot like Stourton promotion was very slow — it needed retirement or someone to snuff it! And everyone knew the next man to retire. We rarely got much in the way of extra work which was always given to Holbeck. We got stuff they didn't want. So when a vacancy at Farnley depot was advertised, I applied and was subsequently transferred to Farnley as a driver.

The work at Farnley was about 60 per cent passenger and all the jobs, with one exception, were the same way out of Leeds, via Morley. Each job started with a climb, which meant the fireman getting stuck in to start with, then straight into a tunnel. Every job we had at Farnley meant tunnels and some were long ones, Morley and Standedge to mention two of them. The class of work at Farnley was more enjoyable than at Stourton. What I found also was not only a change of scenery, but friends and a whole lot of new dialects to master. Leaving behind the numerous Scottish dialects at Carlisle, I was trying to master Liverpool Scouse — it was a most intriguing experience. For a time at Farnley I was 'spare' driver. This meant learning every route at the shed! — Leeds to Liverpool via Stalybridge and Manchester as well as Stockport and Blackpool. The different routes to Blackpool were so numerous it was like a spider's web.

By this time the 'Super Ds' had largely been superseded by the 'Austerities' and Class 8s. The passengers were mainly worked by 'Black 5s'. 'Five Xs' were not quite as efficient on this route — owing to the size of the wheels they had a bit of difficulty getting off the mark — but Farnley did have four or five of them. We also worked a few 'Royal Scots', Liverpool engines. The 'Scots' were a very good engine, both for the fireman and driver, but for one thing. Owing to the low window and the high seat, a driver had to sit down to drive them and as I do not suffer from 'ducks disease' I just could not put my head out. It was a case of either cold head and shoulders or keep right in and try to peer through the front window, which soon got mucked up. You found that if you kept your head in when at speed, like from Marsden to Huddersfield, the cab would lurch and you got a nice belt on your head from the cab side.

One of my first driving jobs on express trains at Farnley was on the 10.42 p.m. York-Bangor mail. Now, at Stourton, in the twenty years I was there, the number of passenger trains I had worked as a driver could be counted on one hand and I had never worked one in the dark. The mail was double-headed from Leeds to Stalybridge; we were in the train engine and the pilot was manned by Patricroft men on their way home. We set off and, believe me, the road took on a complete change. We seemed to be flying. I was striving to see my landmarks but the smoke and the rolling made things a bit of a problem. My mate kept looking at me and grinning his head off, 'You'll soon get used to it mate.' Up the bank from Huddersfield and into the tunnel. At Marsden we got the tank filled on the troughs, then out like a cork from a bottle and down the Micklehurst line. There was a row of houses that was coming up very fast towards us and for a moment I was wondering which side we would pass them! At the end of that shift I really felt great. We worked the newspaper train back and when we booked off I knew I had at last made the grade.

The bit of railway from Huddersfield to Stalybridge is worth a mention as it is quite an interesting section. After leaving the two short tunnels it begins the gentle climb up the valley and gets more lovely as it does so. On the other side the A62 road keeps pace on the way to the top. Approaching Marsden, the hillside rises steeply with the tall masts of the Moorside Edge Radio Station towering up. The hill is so steep one wonders how the farms and cottages stay put and don't roll down. In fact it is typical 'Last of the Summer Wine' country and truly a beautiful part of the Pennines. The railway from Huddersfield had both a slow and a fast line to Standedge Tunnel which was unique in having water troughs inside it. The fast lines went into single 'holes' and as you shot in, everything went black and still! The smoke and steam swirled into the cab giving an eerie feeling of motionlessness, then the sulphurous fumes and heat came over you. You began to sweat. As the walls of the tunnel were so close all around you, it muffled the sound too. There was only the roll and feel of your own loco to remind you that it was still moving. The fireman released the chain on the water scoop handle and then waited. About a mile from the end a gong sounded. He dropped the scoop, the driver watched the gauge and as soon as it reached the top he popped the whistle and the fireman on the front loco dropped his scoop in. Thus, both engines got a full tank, providing the train was moving fast enough. The slow line had a double tunnel which is still in use. The smoke and fumes were not quite as bad but they were bad enough. Leaving the tunnel, the railway forked — the right-hand to Greenfield and Mossley. The left fork was the fast line via Micklehurst which went on the opposite side of the valley and joined up with the other just outside Stalybridge in Stalybridge Tunnel (yes, another tunnel!). The scenery then loses out to a more industrial scene.

Throughout my railway career I have had more than my fair share of really good mates. The firemen I have had were not only good at their job but were, for the most part, comedians too. It made my job so much easier. In fact, there was one time, during a long weekend, when my missus said, 'I think you can't wait to get back to work!' Well, that was not really true, but I don't think many people know the depressing feeling of going to work when everyone else is going out to the theatre or cinema and pubs and clubs. I have had to leave friends, apologising, to get some bed (about four hours) in order to be fresh for work. This was not just occasionally but regularly, Christmas and holidays too, so I thank my luck in having had such good mates. It made the conditions far more acceptable.

Railwaymen are by reputation tea drinkers. I was and still am a big one. I had a good tutor as my father also was a tea-drinking loco man. At work we had pint tea cans and one of my first firemen was also a big tea drinker. We not only had cans, but always carried a cup in our pockets to be ready when anyone else mashed. We were good tea bandits!

Like any shed with freight jobs, there was the usual relieving in the relief cabins, at Huddersfield, Stockport and Manchester. I recall going in to the cabin at Edgeley (Stockport) to wait for the train from Mold Junction. We decided it was time to have our 'bait' or 'snap'. This cabin was, as usual, fairly dull. We sat at the table.

'Shall I mash Bill?'

'O.K. Don.'

Donald went to the geyser. A moment later he came to the table, then, 'Damn!'

'What's the matter?'

'I've forgotten to warm the can before I mashed.'

'You forgot? You've made a mess of that. I can't sup that!'

Immediately, Don went to the sink and emptied the can. He came back, after refilling it.

'That's better.'

Throughout, we both had straight faces. The driver and guard sitting at our table looked at each other and then at us. The driver said to me, 'Your mate threw that can of tea away just because he didn't warm it first?'

'Of course he did,' I said, 'he knows that I wouldn't drink it without it was warmed first.'

'The pair of you are bloody crackers!'

What he didn't know was that Don had forgotten to put the mashing in and saw it on the table when he got back. What he threw away was hot water. I didn't know myself at the time, but I would always play along with him for the laugh. This sort of situation was too good to let go. The expressions on the faces of the men around us were a picture.

It was about this time that I had another scary experience. We had been relieved at Huddersfield on a freight train. 'Your train is over on the goods line Bill. The men had a train to catch home, so I've kept an eye on it,' said the loco foreman. We walked across; as we went down the train we glanced through the slots at the sides of the doors. It was a brilliant moonlit morning and we could see the sky through every one.

'They look like empties, Bill.'

'Aye, they do.'

The loco was an 'Austerity'. We released the brake and rolled off as it is downhill at Huddersfield. We got the distant for the Leeds New line and then opened up. The now closed New line climbed via

Gomersal Tunnel to Birstall, then over the top and down via Gildersome Tunnel to Farnley Junction and Copley Hill sidings. As we began to climb the train started feeling heavy, so we had to get stuck in a bit. My mate said, 'I bet the ruddy guard has got his brakes on', but we just bashed on into Gomersal Tunnel where the smoke and fumes followed you, again giving the feeling of being stationary. The heat and blast off the tunnel roof from the chimney was very noxious and things could get quite unpleasant to say the least, especially when working heavy goods trains. On quite a few trains it was a case of tying a wet handkerchief round your face, bandit style. The pall hung so thick and heavy that it was possible, at times, to bend down and look under it. At times like this the tunnel seemed endless. By the time we came out, we were both coughing and spluttering something cruel. It was grand to fill our lungs with fresh air, the stuff we take so much for granted. 'I'll have a word or two with our guard when we get to the sidings,' I muttered. At Birstall we were over the top and could shut off. 'Thank goodness for that,' my mate said and sat down.

Usually with a loaded goods train, this was the place where we had to screw the brake on, but not with an empty wagon train. Also, we were of the opinion the guard had forgotten to take his hand-brake off. I let them run over the top in the normal way, but somehow I had a feeling that it just didn't seem right. I started to apply the brake a little, then I went across and screwed the hand-brake on too. The 'Austerities' had combination brakes, that is both vacuum and straight steam brake. Also they had a clock that showed the steam pressure in the brake cylinders. As we entered Gildersome Tunnel I gave the brake some more, but we didn't seem to be reducing speed at all so I applied it fully. My mate looked across and then got his foot on the tender end and heaved a bit more on the hand brake. I looked at the brake clock. It showed nearly 200 and the engine was blowing off at just over 200 and was getting all the pressure in the brake. 'I've been in this mess once before,' I said to myself. This time there was nothing wrong with the loco so on with the sanders. In the tunnel the noise was deafening. I was winding into back gear, the wheels kept locking and sparks lit up the tunnel like bonfire night. Once again, I was not frightened but more worried. What could I do now?

At the end of the tunnel was the distant for Gildersome. It was on in accordance with the regulations as the next section was Farnley Junction, which was a big and very busy junction. I began whistling short, sharp pops, my mate still swinging hard on the hand brake. It is surprising how much wear can come off the tender blocks at speed. We shot out of the tunnel, the signalman was at the window, the signals were off. Not that it made any difference, we couldn't do anything about it.

'The road levels out a bit by the starter for about a hundred yards, we may get a hold then. If not, get ready to bail out!' I told my mate. There had been a big smash here a few years before I went to Farnley. There were a few killed and some burned. The smash was between a petrol train and a passenger — I was determined that neither myself nor my mate were going to share the statistics.

As I had hoped, the bit of level track had the desired effect. We got the train under control. I kept the engine in back gear and we just crept into Copley Hill sidings. I got down and went straight back to the guard who was walking steadily towards me, evidently at peace with the world.

'Hello Bill, how's things?'

'Things! What's wrong with this train?'

'Oh, have you brought us in? Where did you get on?'

I told him. And I told him the bother we had had. 'I've never known a train of empties drag like this.'

'Empty!' he exclaimed, 'Take a look at these!' With that, we both climbed up and in the wagons were sheets of metal.

'What are they?'

'Copper plate!' he said.

If the man whom we had relieved had not been in too big a hurry to get off, he would have told me to take the New line only with a double-header, otherwise the old line via Dewsbury and Morley. Well, all's well that ends well and it was just another bit of experience I suppose.

Another important thing happened to me at Farnley. The Branch Secretary of the Union I belonged to was about to retire and asked me if I would like to take over. I accepted and thus increased my sphere of friends and acquaintances. Every new venture I have undertaken has produced its moments and the trade union side was no exception. As branch secretary I was also the local grievance committee, so at any time I was allowed into the inner sanctum of the foreman's office. I went into the office one afternoon and in there was the senior foreman with the running shed foreman facing him at the other side of a large table which had all the rosters and telephones on it. They were looking rather apprehensive for some obscure reason, but I sailed in completely oblivious to what was going on.

'Now then Joe, what about the ...'

I was cut short by the phone ringing in front of me. I still didn't see the almost scared look that came over them, but I can see it now! I picked up the receiver.

'Central office of information,' I said.

'Is that Farnley shed?'

'Right cock! First time. This is the nerve centre of the industry!'

There was a pause and the expression on the faces of my colleagues was a mixture of horror, shock and, at the same time, bursting with laughter. Then suddenly I thought an atom bomb had gone off at the other end of the phone.

'Who the !*?&*! is that and what are you talking about? Put the foreman on. I'll deal with you later!'

It was the District Motive Power Superintendent, speaking from York where he had been to get a telling off in no uncertain manner. Like the army when anything thing goes wrong, each person gives the rocket to his underling (that's what an underling is for, to take the blame). On the railway it is the same, only I had stepped in and broken the chain, which only stoked things up and made them a little worse.

The mate I had for the longest period of all was Cliff. He was not only an excellent fireman but a very good driver, so we alternated driving and firing. He was my fireman for three and a half years and had a sense of humour second to none — as did his wife. We had just worked a heavy goods train and got relieved at Brighouse. We went into the small hut which served as a relief cabin — it had a couple of tables and forms providing seating for about twelve to fifteen blokes. We opened the door and the heat nearly felled us, but steam locomen could stand anything, we had to, so we washed and mashed and sat down to have our well-earned snap. I got out my sandwiches, packed neatly by my 'beloved'. Cliff got his bag on to the seat and lifted out his parcel of sandwiches. He unwrapped them, then shouted, 'The barmy bugger. I'll kill 'er when I get 'ome!' In his paper there was a neat pile of potato peelings, old cabbage stalks and apple skins! The entire place was in uproar, laughing. Needless to say, there was his snap underneath, well wrapped up.

The New line from Farnley Junction had a very severe gradient and freight trains were banked to the top at Birstall. A bank engine would push until the train had cleared the tunnel at Gildersome, then ease off gently to enable the leading engine to 'pick 'em up'. If the banker shut off too quickly it would give the guard a severe snatch or even break a coupling. Banking was a rough job. The worst part of the bank was in the tunnel so the bloke on the banker got the full benefit of the muck and sulphurous fumes from the other engine. The smoke was usually pretty bad. The guard lit the side lights but it was almost impossible to see them. The only thing you saw were the sparks from the chimney top. As the freight pulled out of the sidings, the driver on the banker would note the train man, 'Oh, its 'im. He won't pull much.' And the train driver would see who was his banker, 'Oh, it's that idle sod. We look like having to pull his share as well as our own.'

Most of the heavy freight trains were at night. On one occasion one of the lazy types went up behind and they set off up the bank and into the tunnel. The fireman said, 'This is a light train mate!' It certainly was. As they came out into the lovely starry night they were on their own. The train they were supposed to be pushing had 'pushed off'!

I was on a heavy job and we signalled for the banker. 'It's that idle joker, Bill.' We set off and sure enough were having quite a struggle, slipping and starting and sweating. Then my mate said, 'Right, now then Bill. I'll show you a little trick that might work.' He went to the shovel plate of the tender and thereupon 'made water' on the shovel and a small amount of coal. 'Open the doors, Bill!' I did so and he slung the mess in! Oh boy! It gave off the most evil stench. We just got a quick whiff, but it was enough. It would fill the tunnel behind us. About two minutes elapsed, then what a surge! It worked. The men on the banker couldn't get through quickly enough. These are tricks you hesitated to use, even on your enemy, as it could back-fire and you might be on the banker later!

Some of the jobs that gave me the most pleasure and satisfaction were the Blackpool excursions. They were also very rewarding financially. They were usually Saturday and Sunday jobs which we 'short rested', about five hours off, then worked back. These were trains of people out to enjoy themselves, choose what, and the back-chat we got, both arriving and departing, was great fun. With the working men's club trips it meant crates of beer to go with and restocking to come back. At Blackpool Central the organisation was tremendous. Imagine handling an average of thirty or forty trains over and above the regular traffic. The arrivals were timed for every ten minutes and the departures, at night and early morning, every five minutes with a ten minute gap now and then to fit in a train from Blackpool North (now the only station in Blackpool). Trains were emptied and reversed straight into the sidings, the next train slipping into the platform as near as possible on time. Normal trains included regular service to and from London Euston, but now I'm afraid all that has gone, along with the enormous revenue from excursions, eroded on some flimsy excuse. The coach operators have been handed a real 'golden gift', along with a perfectly situated area to park their cars and coaches — the Central railway station.

7.   The Diesel Age

THE Beeching Plan did much harm and very little if any good to the railway industry. The damage Dr. Beeching inflicted was irreparable. He not only closed stations and remote branch lines, he closed useful sidings, goods lines and slow lines that were in regular use on the pretence of saving maintenance costs. The figures on paper were supposed to justify this action. This was simply not true, as any practical railwayman will tell you. Even today we are having to put up with this folly and on any station on most days one may hear, 'Due to circumstances beyond our control...', 'Due to mechanical failure...', and another classic, 'Due to the slow running of the preceding train...'. These are for the most part unforgivable excuses which would not have to be made but for the closure of various lines and goods lines. It is now often impossible to pass a train that is having difficulty or has come to grief, so the inevitable happens — the job grinds to a halt, with the added difficulty of trying to get some assistance to the failed train. In fact, Dr. Beeching removed the guarantee of an efficient railway system.

Leeds has always been a big centre for the engineering and tailoring trades and the workforce commutes in from the surrounding areas in very large numbers. They come from places like Barnsley, Knottingley and Normanton. These passengers provided quite a large income and the subsequent closures of the stations and branch lines was an act of foolishness. Moves are now being made to re-open or rebuild some of them — the cost will no doubt be more than the closures saved.

In steam days, these trains consisted of non-corridor stock. It was a work of art trying to run them to time and a positive nightmare for the porter and guard to get the trains away. At Normanton, two minutes before time, the porter would walk down the train closing the doors. He would turn round and two or three would be open again. This was repeated until a band of girls came strolling down the platform. The guard opened the first door to get them in quickly, but not on your life! They were getting in with their mates, as they had done for years. Their bus was late but their mates made sure we didn't leave without them. Similarly, at the next stop, Altofts, a colliery village suburb of Normanton, where the station is situated on the top of a high embankment, the performance was repeated if the approaching bus was anywhere in view. In no way could the porter get the doors closed until all was safely gathered in!

Not only is Leeds a big manufacturing city, but it has always had some very good secondary and grammar schools and quite a lot of the pupils travel by rail. Going to school they are little trouble but coming home in those days they would lead the guard a dog's life. When we arrived at the terminus it was a cert that the brake wouldn't come off, there would be at least three communication chains pulled and inside the compartments, the graffiti!! Very often there would be footprints, neatly done, from one side of the compartment to the other, on the ceiling. I can quite understand where the material for St. Trinians came from! Fortunately, the diesel units have put a stop to that caper but the regular passengers still insist on occupying the same seats, day in day out.

In 1960 some drivers at Farnley were sent on a diesel training course at York. The reason was that Gateshead had been allocated some English Electric Type 4s and was to use them on the Newcastle-Liverpool expresses, and as we worked these trains from Leeds we were to be part of the scheme. As I was a senior driver in the Extra Link, I was one of the first to be sent. Diesels were not new — in fact in 1934 there were diesel shunts working in Hunslet goods yard — but main line diesels were things we had only heard about and rarely seen. Some of us had been trained earlier on the '204s' just for one job, to re-lay Morley Tunnel. Owing to its length it was thought that these lively diesels would be just the job.

The training at York was a three week course and it speaks well for the instructors that it was rare that anyone failed, considering that some drivers were in their sixties, practically weaned on steam locomotives and certainly viewed diesels as a passing phase. The course was quite an intensive one as was the exam after it. The inspector said to us, 'We must satisfy ourselves that you know your diesels because when you are out on the road, anyone apart from you that can help is few and far between.' There are about forty things which can cause a fault!

It was also a well planned course. The first day we spent just looking round the thing — it was the first time most of us had seen a diesel at close quarters. The rest of the week we spent in the classroom. We studied charts of the brake system, the air system and the fuel system, then we spent a full day learning the electrics, the fuses and relays, etc. The second week we went into the yard and did the same as we had done in the classroom but this time on the real thing. The final week was spent actually running, with an empty train, between York and Newcastle. We were in two groups of three, each with an inspector who kept putting faults on while we were on the job, so we got the full treatment. At the end of the course we were whacked. After a couple of weeks we were examined and I was taken on a passenger from York to Lincoln and back.

In spite of the intensive training programme it was still possible to have some fun and we did a fair amount of leg pulling with one or two of the inspectors, who took it in good spirit. In fact I think some of them welcomed it. About two weeks after the Type 4 school, two of us were told, 'you two report at the diesel school at Leeds Central for railcar training.' 'What? we are even sweating diesel!', but we went. The bloke who went with me was the crown prince of comedians so it looked like being an interesting course. We duly presented ourselves at the class and were sitting comfortably, when in walked the inspectors. They slowly looked around, 'Let's see what sort of shower we have got this time. Oh bloody hell, it's them two! I'd split them two if I were you George, we had enough of them at York!' Then they cleared off. 'How nice of them to remember us!' said Boothy, my mate.

The railcars were comparatively easy to learn after the Type 4s. Most of the work was finding out where the bits and pieces were situated. This course was one week in the classroom and one week on the road — we really enjoyed it as we were top side of it, but the others in the class were not so fortunate. They were being introduced to diesel traction for the first time. One of the inspectors was a bit of a knowledge box, not very well liked, but I had no trouble with him. As usual, the last days were to be devoted to fault finding.

'We are going to put a few faults on for you so stay put after your snap.' Snap-time came and went, but both the inspectors seemed engrossed in some private conversation while we peasants sat at the far end, waiting.

'Bill, shall we put a few on for them?' said Boothy.

'O.K.', I said, and we dropped down and walked round the unit, isolating and switching off anything and everything, then we climbed back up and sat down again.

After a while, one of the inspectors came to us. 'Sorry chaps, we haven't time for faults. We'll try and fit some in tomorrow. The dolly (signal) is off so we are right for Darlington.'

It was the turn of Jack, a quiet sort of bloke. He knew we had done something, but he didn't know what. Poor Jack — he was not too well up on diesels so little wonder he looked so apprehensive as he sat at the controls. He switched on, the inspector beside him, but nothing happened, no lights, no anything.

The inspector tried the switch and a worried look came over his face. It's one thing to put a fault on that you know about, but this was a different matter entirely. He stood up and stared around, taking a good look at Boothy and me. 'It's you two buggers been at it!'

The expression on his face was alarming. I thought he was going to be ill. Well, it was no good trying to explain so we got down again and started to put things back. It is an easy job to uncouple some things, but a different job to find them and put them right, so it took a little longer than we expected and by the time we were ready we had lost our 'path' to Darlington. This did little to endear us to the inspector, who threatened to 'take it out of us'. History repeated itself. Boothy and Bill were branded.

After the railcar class, the foreman had me in his office. 'Bill, I want you to go with the inspector to pass on the units. If you pass we would like you to work a new kind of railcar, the Trans-Pennine, on its trials.'

I passed and for the next eight or nine weeks I was working between Leeds and Liverpool with the new Trans-Pennine units, a Hull driver working Leeds to Hull. The culmination of the trials was to be a trip to Liverpool with the General Manager of the Eastern Region with his wife and all the top brass and their staff. A very big occasion! I was introduced to them on the platform before starting, the unit being brought in to me. Normally I would have gone to the sidings myself and checked it out. In the cab with me was Jack Anderson, one of the nicest of blokes to work with, so it looked like a promising day. The station master, in full uniform, started us off fifteen minutes before the Newcastle to Liverpool express.

We set off, with my times in front of me. It was vital to obey the slightest speed restriction as the timings were set to the nearest half minute. The train was full of gaffers and I could imagine them sitting there with their watches in their hands. There was also an engineer in the back cab, watching the instruments which duplicated those at my end. It was worse than being a goldfish! As we left the station there was a 5 m.p.h. speed limit, so I glanced at the speedo. It wasn't working!

'Jack, the speedo has failed!' I croaked.

'What! Now?'

'Don't worry Jack', I said, 'I'll keep time. I've been over this road often enough with steamers and no speedos.'

But as we climbed out of Leeds onto the viaduct, I heard the noise of something creaking and crackling. I dropped the window and sure enough the leading bogie wheels were skidding, with sparks and smoke rising. Jack stuck his head out. 'Whoa, Bill!' he yelled. I whoa-ed.

To stop in a section is a very serious situation. The signalman has to be informed as soon as possible so that he can stop the traffic on the other line. Immediately, Jack was down and under the car in no time at all. About three or four fitters materialised from nowhere and about a dozen heads stuck out. The G.M. had been sitting just behind me; I could almost feel the heat of his cigar on my neck. He adjourned to the rear of the train. I don't think he could bear the sight of all the panic going on.

We got on our way again after about twelve minutes, although it was obvious that the tyres had been slightly damaged. We got to Huddersfield, our stop. 'Give the guard a buzz and then set off Bill,' which we did. As we went up the bank, the Chief Engineer came through and after a word with Jack it was decided to cut the run short and stop at Stalybridge. We shunted out of the way of the express and lo and behold, an attendant came into the cab with a tray. 'Coffee and biscuits for the driver.' Boy!! That was one for the book. It was the first time I had had anything like that.

While we were feeding, the cab door was opened from the outside and a very wet, bedraggled bloke climbed in, his lovely white shirt a mess. He was one of the engineers. It seemed he had decided to examine the tyres for himself and, being a gaffer, didn't think it was necessary to tell the staff. He had simply got down when we stopped at Huddersfield but then we suddenly sailed away and left him! Just at that moment, it had started to rain ..... and heavily. It was a suicidal thing to do. What could have happened if that man had looked under doesn't bear thinking about. He was very fortunate.

Eventually I was passed to drive no less than twelve different types of diesel, including 'Deltics' and the High Speed Train, and no extra rate was paid for it. It mattered not whether a man was trained on one or more, the wage was the same. It was a fair way really. Human nature being what it is, some blokes came back after the first couple of days of diesel training and enlarged on the difficulties and faults which put a bit of wind up some chaps, particularly those on shed and local work. It got so bad it could be likened to waiting at the dentists. It really got to one chap. After the first day in class, he went sick and finished up having a nervous breakdown. He was off work, seriously ill, for twelve months.

The main line diesels were a far cry from the old Paxman Rickardo shunting engine that was sent to Stourton in the late thirties. It was a very strong loco and it was put to work on the heaviest shunt in Stourton Down Sidings. It was set in second gear all the time as no-one had the training to work it — we were just shown by the man who was there when it came. It was accepted with suspicion. The older drivers could see the beginning of one-man locos and were against that at all odds. The engine would work for a full week on twenty-four hour shunts, then be brought into the shed for fuel. The rough handling that it received was really criminal. The instructions were vague about the working of it, so there was no hesitation. When the loco wanted reversing the lever was shoved over, without waiting for the engine to come completely to a stop, as is the proper way if damage is to be avoided. Another thing was the dead-mans' pedal. It is illegal to obstruct or interfere with this in any way, but on this joker the pedal was jammed down and secured with a 'Harry Lauder' brake block. Every month, or sooner if the drivers put it out of action, a fitter from Paxmans would come and service the locomotive.

After passing an exam on the Type 4s, we at first seldom had a chance to work one. It was nearly twelve months until my chance came. 'Bill, you are trained on diesels, there's one coming that wants fetching into the shed.' I had to take a steam engine out to change over with the diesel. It was dark and as I got into the loco, it was as if I had never been in one before as training is always done in daylight. I soon got my bearings and got to the shed. As I had reversed in I sent the fireman to set the road while I changed ends to see where I was going. 'O.K. Bill, come on!' I took off the brake and opened the controller. Nothing happened. Well, nothing that should have! Instead, I got the feeling that we were moving backwards. I stuck my head out — we were! I changed back to the other end and drove it into the shed without any trouble, then I examined the loco to see why it behaved as it had. Since we had done our training on them, they had been fitted with an Automatic Warning System with a detachable handle, so I learned about it the hard way!

There was a turn at Farnley on which we worked an express to Liverpool and then travelled to Patricroft for a loco to work the 12.20 a.m. newspaper train to Leeds. As we had little time we travelled in the 'rear cab' of the diesel and had our snap in privacy. To be comfortable I sat on my folded mac on the desk and my mate, Cliff, sat in the driving seat with his feet up. At Leigh we were in the station a short time and could hear a horn blowing, intimating a non-stop train approaching.

'I say Bill, this train doesn't seem to be getting any nearer.'

Then, suddenly, the door was wrenched open and a very angry platform inspector appeared. 'What the hell is going on?'

We both looked at him.

'Who's blowing the ruddy horn?'

It was Cliff. His foot had slowly moved down and was resting on it! The train proceeded and after a while the guard came in to us.

'I might have known you two were on. Which of you keeps switching the lights on and off?'

'What lights?' I said.

He looked at me. 'Them that you are sat on!'

It seemed that I had sat on the switch and every time I moved one way I turned them out; as I turned back, on they came again! Talk of playing by ear!

I often drove the 'Deltics' which have a special place among enthusiasts. They were without a doubt a grand machine for the job for which they were built. The acceleration was terrific. From a driver's point of view they were very noisy and there was not much room to move in the cab, nor in the engine room. In fact it was a side shuffle to move in the engine room at all. The Secondmen were not very keen when working a train that was steam heated as the generator was situated between the two engines and any regulating required when running was to say the least uncomfortable. We were supplied with ear protection in the form of wadding, which we were supposed to twist into plugs but not with our dirty hands. We managed without. Now the majority of trains use electric heating which is a big improvement. The draught on 'Deltics' was terrible. In winter I used to wrap my railway mac or overcoat round my legs, like a tight skirt, and on arrival at the destination it took a minute or two before circulation started again. The draught problem was later rectified and it became a pleasure to work them.

Until the H.S.T. the 'Deltic' was the only loco capable of speeds of 100 mph, but the rolling stock for the most part was limited to 90 mph. There is quite a lot of fantasising about the figure of 100 mph and how fast steam trains can and did travel. Comparisons are made over the time it took a steam train to travel between two points and how long it takes a diesel. There are simple answers. First, there were generally no speedos on steamers, so to judge a speed of say 30 mph accurately was difficult. Generally, the practice in order to comply with a speed limit of 30 mph was just to shut off and freewheel, while 15 mph meant rub the brake a little. With a diesel we could not get away with anything less than spot-on as the clock was staring at you.

The diesel era was now with us and anyone like myself, who had any length of service on steam, would tell you that the change was very welcome. It meant that we could come home after a full shift and not be as black as a sweep and not half as tired. Also, something I had always wanted was to wear a collar and tie without choking, and something that Midland men had never had was an upholstered seat instead of a wooden one. (Some L.N.E.R. engines always had them.) The best thing of all was to be in a warm and comfortable cab and very good all-round vision was a real luxury.

There are few drivers who have done any length of service on steam engines who were not glad they have been replaced. The glamour of the steam locomotive is all on the outside.

8. Vandalism

ALL SHEDS have runs along stretches of line known as 'Bomb Alley' and Farnley was no exception. Leeds to Manchester had more than a small share. Children just can't resist the temptation of doing things they shouldn't and going where it's dangerous, not only to themselves but to others also. In stations where spotters are allowed, they congregate at the end of platforms. Before long there is skylarking with the heavy, four-wheeled barrows and inevitably a barrow finishes up on the track. They are capable of causing a derailment, but drivers are aware of the possibility and keep an eye open for them. Another thing that is common is that these apparently innocent spotters sit on the platform having their sandwiches, with their legs dangling over the platform edge. The clearance is sometimes as little as nine inches and there is a real danger of them losing a limb. Something they rarely understand is that the roads in a station are generally used by both up and down trains.

Where the railway runs through a housing estate, it is almost certain that someone will make a way through the fencing and it is not always a child. Quite often it is an adult who wants a short cut to the pub or club or bus stop. But it is always children who take advantage of the opening to explore and find a new area to play not always innocent games. Another thing about railways is that they pass houses. The railway cuttings are used by the residents as a dumping ground for the sort of rubbish that won't go into a dustbin, such as old bedding and garden refuse, not to mention dead animals! It goes without saying that there are loads of stones and bricks, but this is the material that the children find in their exploratory expeditions and then use to start building booby traps for the trains to run over. In my time I have run over everything imaginable.

When caught, the only thing the children say is that they did it to see what would happen. Well, what happens is not always foreseeable. For instance, what they don't think about is that some things can't be squashed and certain stones, like the flint stones from the ballast, burst. Tiny pieces fly off like bullets and children are at risk just standing near 'To see what happens'. Also, when children are bending down in the 'four foot' they don't leave themselves much time or space to get out of the way. At 60 mph a train needs at least three-quarters of a mile to stop and in the panic to get out there is more than an even chance that they will slip. There are no sprinters who use loose ballast! A locomotive has no steering wheel, so it's the chance of at least a lost limb. A diesel weighs anything from 70 to 100 tons. A most distressing thing about vandalism by children is that they usually do things as a dare or challenge and younger children copy what they have seen their elders do. Quite often the victims are below school age. They get on the permanent way and as the train approaches they don't know how to get out the way. To the driver, the child looks just like a bit of rag until he is very near. His main job is to look for signals.

One Sunday afternoon I was working a D.M.U. and as I ran over a river bridge I disturbed a couple of youths bending over the track. They jumped up, startled, then started their mad dash to get out of the way. There was a wall at each side and they made it with yards only to spare. Had they slipped I would have run over them.

I am certain many parents are unaware of where their children go to play. If they saw some of the places they go and things they do, I think there would be many more causes of heart attack. One day I was on my way to Manchester with a steam express and we were charging down the Greenfield line. Our 'Five X' was blowing off and there was smoke and steam coming from all over. 'Look at that lot, Bill!' 'That lot' was three small children, the eldest would not be older than 10 or 11. They were walking over the line on a round service pipe which bridged the railway and making up the procession was an Alsatian dog!

The 'Bomb Alley' on this road was between Ordsall Lane and Patricroft. Just leaving Manchester for Liverpool the line runs in a cutting between some blocks of flats. Stones and bricks were thrown at trains from both sides simultaneously and also dropped from the road bridges. There was a period when drivers refused to drive a loco to Patricroft shed tender-first as they had no protection. On one of the test runs I made with the Trans-Pennine diesels, I came round the corner at Orsall Lane and was building up speed to 60 mph when a loco inspector who was riding with me suddenly jumped up and shouted, 'Hold tight Bill!' There in front, looped over the track, was what appeared to be half a steel tyre off a wagon wheel. There wasn't anything to do but hang on. It turned out to be an old car tyre, so we breathed a sigh of relief.

Nearer Liverpool, approaching Rainhill, the railway passes through a big estate. I came up a slight rise on to it; the sun was in front of me and causing the rails to shine. Suddenly the left one lost its shine; it looked as if it had been removed. The feeling that comes over you in these situations is horrible. You are cold at the back of your neck, the hair seems to be creeping up, you are sweating. All this happens so quickly. Not until I was about two hundred yards or so away did I realise that someone had laboriously covered the whole rail with earth. It didn't stop us having a most rough and rolling passage but I was thankful that's all it was.

Finally, on the Liverpool road, the railway goes into a deep cutting from Edge Hill into Lime Street station under several high, brick-built bridges. Now this is a real 'Bomb Alley'. The station shunt has a really scary time of it. I have actually seen a children's pram come floating through the air to smash up on the fast line. Old prams are always being dumped in railway cuttings when the shunt is stationary. The driver is always careful to avoid stopping under bridges so that he is not a sitting target.

These are not isolated incidents. They are a few that immediately spring to mind. At this period there had been no fatal injuries to railwaymen — that happened later. I was on the platform at Stalybridge as a Trans-Pennine ran in from Manchester. 'Here, Bill!' said the driver. I went over to him and he pointed at the front of the car. There, still stuck in the direction indicator, was a brick. The glass was still cracking! It had been dropped from a bridge. If it had landed a few inches higher he would certainly have sustained very serious injuries. The most significant thing was that it was his 65th birthday and he retired at the weekend.

In June 1964 the last straw came as I was working a similar train, coming round a corner after leaving Droylsden. As I approached a road bridge I noticed a thick rope looped rather loosely under the bridge. I was doing about 45 mph. As I passed, I just caught sight of a youth holding a large object on the end of the rope which he swung at the train. Misjudging the speed of the train, the weight hit the side, about three windows behind me, causing a thump and startling the passengers. I stopped at Stalybridge and reported the incident. When I booked off duty that day, I went to the foremans' office and stated, 'Jim, I'm just about fed up to the teeth with all this vandalism. It's about time something was done. It needs a driver and a railway policeman to visit the schools around their own sheds.'

'Well Bill, I can't do anything, but if you want to, call in the gaffers' office on your way home.'

This I did. I tore a strip off and said my piece. The superintendent was sympathetic and said, 'Yes, Bill, I understand the problem and I will submit your remarks to head office at York.'

Thus started another very significant part not only of my railway career but of my life. For about four months I heard nothing, then I was told to report to the Regional Manager's office at York. I duly presented myself there and was given a warm reception. We chatted a while until the Public Relations Office assistant arrived. They had noted my comments and decided on a plan, which they put to me, with the remark, 'If we do our part, will you do yours?'

I was put on the spot and could hardly say no. This was the start of what turned out to be a very successful campaign. The idea was to visit the areas where, according to police reports, vandalism was really bad. In the first two years we visited more than two hundred schools, getting our message across to somewhere in the region of two thousand children of all ages. According to the B.T.C. Police, reports of trouble were actually reduced in the areas covered. In the areas we started with, the P.R.O. circulated the information to the press, so we got good coverage. Eventually, we visited all the schools in Castleford, Knottingley, Pontefract, most of Barnsley, Wakefield, Bradford and Leeds, not to mention the surrounding areas and small villages. In fact, any school that was in the vicinity of a railway line.

The exercise was introduced to the children, we showed a couple of interesting railway films, then I would deliver my talk, off the cuff, no script and based entirely on experiences of mine and my colleagues. We finished with a ten minute spell of questions and answers. This was interesting and entertaining. I made it quite plain to the authorities that everything I said to the children was fact and I would not be told what to say. I avoided obviously dangerous things, such as descriptions of how to derail a vehicle. We visited every type of school, from infants of five or six who would rather talk to me than listen, to Secondary and Grammar schools. We became very much in demand as our reputation spread. Some schools asked us to return every year, so that not only the existing pupils got the message but the new ones too. We had a few moving experiences, particularly when visiting special schools for backward children. It was difficult to leave sometimes, as we were besieged by those who were steam enthusiasts.

Some teachers were doubtful whether we were going to make any useful contribution to safety, and one deputy head came to me before we started, saying, 'Don't you think you will be putting ideas in their heads?'

I replied, 'After the talk, ask me that then, also tell me if I have not covered the subject fully.' He was completely on our side afterwards.

The local radio stations have used my services on quite a few occasions, usually when a report has come up concerning accidents on the railway. One highlight came when it was decided to make a film of the exercise. It is an interesting film, but it has lost some of its appeal to railway people because it features steam engines. It was called, appropriately, 'Where do they Play?'

Usually we did not go out of our own region, but occasionally we were asked to visit other areas. This took us to Lincoln, Scunthorpe and once to the little colliery village of Cresswell as the result of an accident. The village was having its annual cricket match and the ground was at the side of a railway embankment. There was a large crowd, with plenty of children in it. It was a Sunday, and no-one thought to restrict the children from playing near the railway line. It only went to the colliery and that was closed on Sunday. It didn't occur to anyone that railways do not close on Sunday. This particular day the ballast train was out, re-laying the branch line. The result was that a child lost its life. My job was to point out how foolish it was to treat a source of danger, like a railway line, with contempt. I was not very popular that day, but vandalism and trespass is a deadly serious thing.

I had to attend a grammar school near Wakefield after an incident in which one of their 'most brilliant pupils' (the head's words) had a leg cut off. I was standing in the corridor, watching the pupils go into the large hall, when, 'Pssst, Mister!' One of the younger ones came to me, looking over his shoulder. 'I know what you've come for. It's about Jonesy. Well, I know what he was doing.' In no time at all, I knew the game of 'dares' he was playing and also the names of the other three who were with him. They were moving wagons in a siding and trying to jump on the buffers for a ride. He missed.

I was paid a very big compliment when a high official from the Southern Region P.R.O. came to a school to hear our talk. The outcome was an invitation to inaugurate a safety campaign against vandalism on that Region.

When I was first giving these talks in 1964 I was in overalls — steam uniform. Then came the first diesel suit, the green one, and after that the 'German Army cap' of today. In the street a railwayman in uniform attracts little attention, but it is different in the classroom. The effect is of being out of context, it is as though they have seen nothing like it. To stand and address an audience of three or four hundred people is a strange experience. The first time I was all for packing the job in! The lump does not come into the throat, it comes in the middle of the chest. I have experienced this on quite a few occasions. It is only really believing in what you are doing that helps you through. If the talks and the time I have devoted to the exercise have been instrumental in saving perhaps only one life, it will have been worthwhile but I shall never know.

9.   Finale

IN 1966 Farnley Junction followed the fate of Copley Hill and closed down. The work and men were transferred to Holbeck which meant the shed was beginning to recoup some mileage after losing so much main line work, such as the London St. Pancras and Glasgow jobs when lodging turns were knocked off. For me, going to Holbeck meant renewing old acquaintances from Stourton and Skipton. It was also the time of other big changes in the area. Leeds station was rebuilt and the original two stations incorporated into one. This was a big operation. Along with two other drivers, I was temporarily promoted to Loco Inspector, to teach men from other depots the new layout and to arrange conductors in and out of the station whilst the change-over was done. This was so that everyone became familiar with the new workings.

Then I moved up into the 'Top Link', the London King's Cross line. This entailed a long and arduous task in learning the road, one I had never seen before or fired over. It took nearly six months. From a scenic point of view the line does not compare with that north to Carlisle, but nevertheless there is plenty of interest if you take the trouble to look for it. First, what struck me was the enormous number of pheasants between Doncaster and Hitchin. Also, in the 185 miles, it was possible to notice how one part of the country was still in the throes of winter and the other enjoying a springtime showing of flowers. Some parts of the route are easily flooded and how picturesque it could be with the evening sun reflecting in the water, particularly around Huntingdon. The autumn sunsets we saw when working the 8.20 p.m. Edinburgh mail from King's Cross were impressive too. These were sights I never tired of seeing. I suppose it was scenes like these that caused me to take up easel and brushes and start oil-painting in 1970 so as to try and put on canvas all the lovely things I have been privileged to see.

In the late 1970s I began driving the High Speed Trains as they came into service. H.S.T.s are so smooth starting and stopping that this created a situation for me I can't say I'm proud to admit. We were waiting at Doncaster for the London to Bradford train—it was late evening and dark. My mate on this occasion was a young lad with about four months' experience, a keen lad nevertheless. The train came, not as booked a Deltic but a H.S.T. My mate was thrilled pink! It was the first time for him. Off we went to Bradford Exchange.

Now, Bradford was on a gradient but it presented no problems as such. We came to a stop about eight feet from the hydraulic buffers, then changed ends in the proper manner. I applied one notch to the brake as laid down in the training schedule, put on the light and started to catch up on writing my driver's sheet. The cab was beyond the platform edge and in the dark. We had stood about five minutes when the telephone buzzed. It was the guard, 'Driver, don't come any nearer the buffers!' I looked across to my mate, 'What's he on about? We haven't moved have we?' 'No, I don't think so.' I carried on writing, then two minutes later the phone buzzed again. 'Driver, you have crashed the buffers and there is someone who wants a word with you.' I applied the brake fully and went back, and sure enough the train had actually crept back very slowly in spite of the brake. The station buffers had pressed through the fibre-glass nose, making two pefectly round holes and coming to rest on the proper buffers inside (not many people know of the existence of these). It had then continued and compressed the plungers on the station buffers before coming to a stop.

Neither of us at the front had had any indication of movement or of stopping. The station manager and staff were quite worked up about the affair. 'Driver, you may have damaged our buffers, so I'll have to report it!' I wasn't concerned about his drop of water in the buffers, I was bothered about why the brake hadn't held as it was supposed to. I took the train to Neville Hill H.S.T. depot and reported to the foreman; the damage was very slight—only the fibre-glass.

The outcome was this. Firstly, it was discovered that the brakes on two of the vehicles were defective and secondly the engineers decided that one notch of the brake would not really be enough to hold on some gradients as we had been instructed, so modifications were made to the units and the class instructions. I don't regard it as anything to my credit that I was the first driver at Holbeck to 'prang' a H.S.T., but being the guinea pig may have prevented a more serious accident.

*　　　　*　　　　*　　　　*

In May 1973 I received a most unusual letter from the Lord Chamberlain's Office. It was an invitation to a garden party at Buckingham Palace! Well, no words could ever describe what my wife and I felt. It was completely out of the blue. What! Why! Who!—I checked to see if it was a mistake. How on earth could this happen to us? Well, it was genuine, then we wanted all the world to know. I had to inform the shed as I would need time off work to attend. The Chief Clerk was nearly as thrilled as we were, then he told me that for occasions such as these the railway company would pay all our expenses—hotel, taxis, the lot. Boy, was I thrilled!

The big day came, the 26th of June 1973. We entered the grounds, my wife on my arm. We just floated in the most beautiful flamingo park, the lake surrounded by flowers and shrubs. We then made our way to the Palace where the guests were beginning to congregate. It was like being in a wonderland of glittering costumes: there were full dress uniforms, complete with medals and swords, Arabs in flowing cloaks and jewelled ornaments, film stars and stage stars in immaculate morning suits and dresses, and politicians with their ladies too. The Beefeaters and Gentlemen at Arms came out to arrange a space for the Royal Party. The Queen's path lay in our direction. As she passed very close it seemed as if she glanced our way which made a very personal moment. It was an experience that my wife and I will treasure for the rest of our lives.

We were in a world of our own for weeks after. We talked about it over and over again, but just as if to test us and see how much excitement a person can stand, in May 1974 came another letter. I had been working on nights. I came downstairs and was met by my wife with an odd look on her face. She handed me a letter, this time from the Prime Minister's office. I had been awarded the British Empire Medal in the June Birthday Honours List. Words again failed me. The big thing about my award was the amount of pleasure and happiness that friends past and present seemed to derive from it. It was well worth while.

Finally, after 46 years' service, I decided to take the opportunity offered to retire. I have had a most enjoyable working life, doing a job I really wanted to do and I have really no regrets. Also I have been privileged to have served through a complete era, starting from steam engines in their heyday then the changeover to diesel traction and finally was able to work to the top of my profession, the H.S.T. service. I have had what is commonly called 'job satisfaction', and to have it all capped with my award, which my wife and family were able to share with me—well, it must make me the happiest and most lucky person around.